LOST SHEPHERD

Lost
Shepherd

HOW POPE FRANCIS IS
MISLEADING HIS FLOCK

Philip F. Lawler

REGNERY GATEWAY

Regnery Gateway™ is a trademark of
Salem Communications Holding Corporation
Regnery® is a registered trademark of
Salem Communications Holding Corporation

Cataloging-in-Publication data on file with the Library of Congress

ISBN 978-1-62157-722-5
e-book ISBN 978-1-62157-753-9

Published in the United States by
Regnery Gateway
An imprint of Regnery Publishing
A Division of Salem Media Group
300 New Jersey Ave NW
Washington, DC 20001
www.RegneryGateway.com

Manufactured in the United States of America

10 9 8 7 6 5 4 3 2

Books are available in quantity for promotional or premium use.
For information on discounts and terms, please visit our website:
www.Regnery.com.

CONTENTS

INTRODUCTION   vii

CHAPTER ONE
The Surprise Election   1

CHAPTER TWO
The Francis Effect   13

CHAPTER THREE
Stalled Reforms   39

CHAPTER FOUR
Manipulating the Synod   73

CHAPTER FIVE
The Unanswered Question   97

CHAPTER SIX
The Document and the *Dubia*   113

CHAPTER SEVEN
Allies and Enemies   145

CHAPTER EIGHT
Tradition in the Balance   173

INDEX   197

E very day I pray for Pope Francis. And every day (I am exagger-
ating, but only slightly), the pope issues another reminder that
he does not approve of Catholics like me.

If the Holy Father were rebuking me for my sins, I would have no
reason to complain. But day after weary day, in his homilies at morning Mass in the Vatican's St. Martha residence, the pope upbraids
me—and countless thousands of other faithful Catholics—for clinging
to, and sometimes suffering for, the truths that the Church has always
taught. We are rigid, he tells us. We are the "doctors of the law," the
Pharisees, who only want to be "comfortable" with our Faith.

In the early days of his pontificate, Francis captured the public
imagination with his call for a new, vigorous, worldwide mission. I was
one of millions caught up in the "Francis effect," enthusiastic about his
vision. I found that friends and neighbors, inspired by what they read
and heard about the pope, wanted to talk with me about the Catholic
Faith: not about the politics of the Vatican or the scandals of the clergy,
but about the fundamental message of the Gospel.

As time passed, however, the tone and even the content of the
pope's public statements puzzled me, then distressed me. For months,
in my work reporting on the daily news from the Vatican, I did my

best to provide reassurance—for my readers and sometimes for myself—that despite his sometimes alarming remarks, Francis was not a radical, was not leading the Church away from the ancient sources of the Faith. But gradually, reluctantly, painfully, I came to the conclusion that he was.

The Roman pontiff should be a focus of unity in the Church. Francis, regrettably, has become a source of division. There are two reasons for this unhappy development: the pope's autocratic style of governance and the radical nature of the program that he is relentlessly advancing.

The autocratic style, which contrasts sharply with promises of collegial and synodal governance, has never been quite so evident as in January 2017, when he tossed aside the independent and sovereign status of an ancient Catholic fraternal order, the Knights of Malta. Writing of that remarkable coup in the *Wall Street Journal*, Sohrab Ahmari observed that it "has divided the church along familiar lines." Ahmari, a recent convert to Catholicism, continued:

> As with other recent disputes—communion for the divorced-and-remarried; the status of the Latin Mass; Vatican engagement with China's Communist regime—conservatives are on one side and Pope Francis is on the other.

But a pope should not be on "one side" of disagreements within the Church. Certainly the Roman pontiff must make decisions and set policies. But unlike a political leader, he is not expected to bring his own particular agenda to his office, to promote his allies and punish his opponents. Whereas we expect President Trump to reverse policies of President Obama—just as Obama reversed policies of President Bush—we expect a pope to *preserve* the decisions of his predecessors. Because the Church is not, or should not be, divided into rival parties.

Every pope makes controversial decisions, and every controversial decision leaves some people unhappy. But a prudent pontiff avoids even the appearance of acting arbitrarily. Mindful that he serves as head of a *college* of bishops—not as a lone monarch—he does his best to *propose* rather than *im*pose solutions to pastoral problems.

Although he exercises enormous authority within the Church, a pope also acts under considerable restraints. He is empowered to speak for the universal Church, but in a sense he forfeits the ability to speak for himself. The pope cannot be partisan. He is expected to settle arguments, not to start them. At the Council of Jerusalem, St. Peter set the standard for his successors: hearing out the arguments on both sides and then rendering a judgment (in this case, ruling *against* the position that he himself had previously held).

By its very nature the pope's role is conservative, in the best sense of that word. He is charged with preserving the purity and clarity of our Faith, a Faith that does not change. Since our fundamental beliefs were set forth by Jesus Christ, no prelate can question them without subverting the authority of the Church that Our Lord founded—the same Church that gives him his only claim to authority. While he is the supreme teacher of the Catholic Faith, the pope can teach only what the Church has always taught: the Deposit of Faith that has been passed down to him from the apostles. He can speak infallibly, but only when he proclaims and defines what faithful Catholics have "always and everywhere" believed.

In short the pope cannot teach something new. He can express old truths in new ways, but if he introduces actual novelties, he is abusing his authority. And if his "new" teachings conflict with the established doctrines of the Church, he is undermining that authority.

Many faithful Catholics believe that with *Amoris Laetitia*, Francis has encouraged beliefs and practices that are incompatible with the prior teachings of the Church. If that complaint is justified, he has violated the sacred trust that is given to Peter's successors. If that complaint is not justified, the Holy Father at a minimum owes us explanations, not insults.

Something snapped inside me on February 24, 2017, when Francis turned the day's Gospel reading (Mark 10:1–12) into one more opportunity to promote his own view on divorce and remarriage.

Condemning hypocrisy and the "logic of casuistry," the pontiff said that Jesus rejects the approach of legal scholars. True enough. But in his rebuke to the Pharisees, what does Jesus say about marriage?

> So they are no longer two but one flesh. What therefore God has joined together, let not man put asunder.

and

> Whoever divorces his wife and marries another, commits adultery against her; and if she divorces her husband and marries another, she commits adultery.

Sometimes, in his homilies, the pope's interpretation of the Scriptures is forced; often his characterization of tradition-minded Catholics is insulting. But in this case, the pope turned the Gospel reading completely upside-down. Reading the Vatican Radio account of that astonishing homily, I found I could no longer pretend that Francis was merely offering a novel interpretation of Catholic doctrine. No, it was more than that. He was engaged in a deliberate effort to change what the Church teaches.

For more than twenty years, writing daily about the news from the Vatican, I had tried to be honest in my assessment of papal statements and gestures. I had criticized St. John Paul II and Benedict XVI when I thought that their actions were imprudent. But never had it crossed my mind that either of those popes posed any danger to the integrity of the Catholic Faith. Looking back much further across Church history, I realized that there had been bad popes, men whose personal actions were motivated by greed and jealousy and lust for power and just plain lust. But had there ever before been a Roman pontiff who disregarded so easily what the Church has always taught and believed and practiced on such bedrock issues as the nature of marriage and of the Eucharist?

Pope Francis had sparked controversy from the day he was elected as St. Peter's successor. But the controversy eventually became so intense, confusion among the faithful so widespread, administration at the Vatican so arbitrary—and the pope's diatribes against his (real or imagined) foes so manic—that today the universal Church is rushing toward a crisis.

In a large family, how should a son behave when he realizes that his father's behavior threatens the welfare of the whole household? He should certainly continue to show respect for his father, but he cannot indefinitely deny the danger. Eventually, a dysfunctional family needs an intervention.

In the worldwide family that is the Catholic Church, the best means of intervention is always prayer. But intervention also requires honesty—a candid recognition that we have a serious problem.

Recognizing the problem can also provide a sort of relief, a relaxation of accumulating tensions. When I tell friends that I consider this papacy a disaster, more often than not they feel oddly reassured. They can relax a bit, knowing that their own misgivings are not irrational, that others share their fears about the future of the Faith, that they need not continue a fruitless search for ways to reconcile the irreconcilable. Moreover, having given the problem a proper name, they can recognize what this crisis of Catholicism is *not* and put aside the explanations offered by some radical traditionalists. Francis is not an antipope, much less the Antichrist. The see of Peter is not vacant, and Benedict is not the "real" pontiff.

Francis is our pope, for better or worse. And if it is for worse—as I sadly conclude it is—the Church has survived problematic popes in the past. We Catholics have been spoiled for decades, enjoying a succession of outstanding pontiffs who were gifted teachers and saintly men. We have grown accustomed to looking to Rome for guidance. Now we cannot.

I do not mean to imply that Francis has forfeited the charism of infallibility. If he issues an *ex cathedra* statement, in union with the world's bishops, we can be sure that he is fulfilling his duty to pass on what the Lord gave to St. Peter: the Deposit of Faith. But this pope has, characteristically, chosen *not* to speak with authority; on the contrary, he has adamantly refused to clarify his most provocative teaching document.

But if we cannot count on clear directions from Rome, where can we turn? First, Catholics can rely on the constant teaching of the Church, the doctrines that are now too often called into question. If the pope is confusing, the *Catechism of the Catholic Church* is not. Second, we can and should ask our own diocesan bishops to step up and shoulder their responsibilities. Bishops, too, have spent years referring the tough questions to Rome. Now, of necessity, they must provide their own clear, decisive affirmations of Catholic doctrine.

Maybe Francis will prove me wrong and emerge as a great Catholic teacher. I hope and pray he does. Maybe my entire argument is wrongheaded. I have been wrong before and will no doubt be wrong again; one more mistaken view is of no great consequence. But if I am right, and the current pope's leadership has become a danger to the Faith, then other Catholics, and especially ordained Church leaders, must decide how to respond. And if I am right that confusion about fundamental Church teachings has become widespread, then the bishops, as primary teachers of the faith, cannot neglect their duty to intervene. The history of the Catholic Church shows that bishops will respond to a clamor from the faithful, and the bishop of Rome, whose task is to unify the brethren, cannot ignore his brother bishops.

CHAPTER ONE

The Surprise Election

L ightning struck St. Peter's Basilica twice on February 11, 2013. Two different photographers captured dramatic pictures of the second bolt lighting up the darkened sky around the dome of the basilica. Those photos served as perfect illustrations for the day's headline story from Rome: the shocking announcement by Pope Benedict XVI that he would resign from the papacy.

The German pontiff broke the news at a consistory—a meeting of the cardinals then in Rome—called for the routine purpose of confirming plans for the canonization of three new saints. Benedict had kept his retirement plans secret, giving prior notice to only a few top Vatican officials. Since he made his stunning announcement in Latin, most members of his audience had difficulty following him. But those who were fluent in the ancient language began to stir when Benedict said, "I have come to the certainty that my strengths, due to an advanced age, are no longer suited to an adequate exercise of the Petrine ministry," and they gasped when he went on to "declare that I renounce the ministry of Bishop of Rome," the resignation to take effect at the end of the month.

The news was electrifying. No Roman pontiff had resigned in more than five hundred years. The last pope to do so voluntarily was

Celestine V, in 1294. The idea that a Vicar of Christ would abdicate his responsibility was shocking to many faithful Catholics. (Celestine would eventually be canonized but only after considerable criticism; he is usually identified as the shadowy character in Canto III of Dante's *Inferno*, "the craven one, who made the great denial.") Benedict had spoken about resignation a few times, as had his predecessor John Paul II, but only as a theoretical possibility. Now it was a reality.

No one had expected a long pontificate for Benedict XVI when he was elected, three days before his seventy-eighth birthday. He had never been robust, having suffered at least one stroke and relying on a pacemaker. His advanced age and frail health, in fact, made some observers doubt that he would be chosen by the conclave of April 2005.

And indeed, the strains of the papacy took an obvious physical toll on Benedict. By 2012, visitors to the apostolic palace reported that although in the morning the pope was as alert as ever, by midday he would grow visibly weary, lose concentration, and need a rest before he could resume productive work. Troubled by arthritic knees, he was less steady on his feet. He was approaching his eighty-fifth birthday.

At the same time, the problems that demanded the pope's attention seemed to grow steadily more intense:

- The sex-abuse scandal that had devastated the Church in the United States a decade earlier was sweeping across Europe. There were angry demands for the resignation of bishops who had failed to take action against abusive clerics. Benedict, who on the eve of his election had decried the "filth" that soiled the Catholic priesthood, had stepped up the Vatican's efforts to remove offenders from ministry.
- European banking inspectors charged that the Vatican bank, known as the Institute for Religious Works, was providing a haven for money laundering. The

Vatican had begun a series of economic reforms, designed to ensure transparency and restore confidence in the institution.

- In the so-called "Vatileaks" scandal, confidential Vatican documents, mostly related to questionable financial transactions, had fallen into the hands of Italian journalists, who used them as the basis for sensational stories. An internal investigation traced the leaks to the pope's own valet, Paolo Gabriele, who was found guilty of aggravated theft by a Vatican tribunal. (A papal pardon spared him from an eighteen-month prison sentence.) But many observers doubted the tribunal's finding that Gabriele had acted alone. It seemed reasonable to speculate that other senior Vatican officials, who had more reason to engage in intramural intrigues, had guided the leaks.

- A special commission of three retired cardinals investigated Vatileaks and delivered its voluminous report to the pontiff at the end of 2012. Although the results of that investigation were never made public, Rome buzzed with rumors, some published in leading newspapers, that the cardinals had uncovered a homosexual network inside the Vatican that exposed prelates to threats of blackmail.

Apparently Benedict had reached the conclusion that he, now an elderly man and by nature and training a scholar rather than an administrator, had neither the strength nor the talent that would be needed to resolve these internal crises. As they gathered in Rome to choose his successor, the world's cardinals were obviously thinking along similar lines. They spoke frequently to reporters about finding a leader with a firm administrative hand who could preside over a much-needed reform of the Vatican bureaucracy.

Looking for a Different Style of Leadership

There were other clear themes, too, in the conversations that preceded the conclave, which was to open on March 12. The cardinals were eager to pursue the "new evangelization" that had been a priority for both John Paul II and Benedict XVI, but they were open to a different style of leadership. During the long pontificate of John Paul II, Cardinal Joseph Ratzinger had been the Polish pontiff's closest aide and confidant. Since he had continued his predecessor's policies when he succeeded him as pope, the Church had in many respects been governed by the same papal regime for thirty-five years. An old Vatican adage has it that a "fat pope follows a thin pope," meaning that a conclave should choose a man with different personal qualities, a different leadership style.

Some cardinals suggested that the time might be ripe for a pope from the Third World. The choice of John Paul II, the first non-Italian pope in centuries, had been a spectacular success. Maybe it was time to look farther afield. Catholicism was making great gains in Africa and South America, while the influence of the Church was waning in Europe.

The argument for a non-European pontiff was strengthened by the absence of an outstanding candidate among the European *papabili*. Cardinal Ratzinger had been the obvious choice going into the conclave of 2005. The world's most influential prelate, he would have been an overwhelming favorite for election but for the questions about his health. In 2013, Cardinal Angelo Scola of Milan was generally regarded as the leading Italian contender, but the field was crowded.

Cardinal Scola may well have been the preferred candidate of the outgoing pope. But Benedict would not participate in the conclave or make any comment at all—about the vote or about the needs of the Church. Having vowed his fidelity to the future pontiff, he departed the Vatican for the papal summer residence at Castel Gandolfo until the new pope was settled in his office. Even after his return, the retired pope would maintain a strict silence about current ecclesiastical affairs.

In the days leading up to a conclave, the world's cardinals, already assembled in Rome, meet in daily "general congregations" that have two purposes. First, since there is no pope to make final decisions during the *sede vacante* period, the cardinals work together on the necessary business of the Holy See. Second, and more important, the cardinals exchange ideas about the needs of the Church—the needs to which the next pope will be asked to respond.

These general congregations are closed to outsiders, and the Vatican press office provides only vague reports about what the cardinals have discussed or decided. For the first few days of the meetings in 2013, the cardinals from the United States held daily briefings, giving the media more information about the talks. But other cardinals complained about what they saw as a breach of confidentiality, and the American prelates reluctantly called off their briefings. Father Federico Lombardi, the director of the Vatican press office, explained that the American cardinals' silence would be in keeping with a general understanding that during the days leading up to a papal conclave, the attitude of the cardinals is "one of reservation in order to safeguard the freedom of reflection on the part of each of the members of the College of Cardinals who has to make such an important decision."

Nevertheless, enterprising Vatican journalists were able to generate reports from the daily congregations. Despite the perception that Vatican affairs are shrouded in secrecy, the rumor mill is always working, and reports about internal discussions invariably leak out into the Italian papers. Even after a papal conclave, at which every cardinal solemnly swears that he will not divulge anything about what happens, reporters usually can give a fairly clear account of the proceedings within a few weeks, and no one doubts that the account is reasonably accurate. During the *sede vacante* period, when the cardinals are living in their own apartments and having dinner conversations with their aides and friends, reporters find it relatively easy to tease out details about the discussions during the congregations.

For example, before the 2013 conclave, an Italian reporter disclosed that the cardinals would be briefed by the three prelates—Cardinals Julián Herranz, Jozef Tomko, and Salvatore De Giorgi—who had prepared the hefty dossier on the Vatileaks scandal for Benedict. Because all three cardinals on the investigating commission were over the age of eighty, none would be participating in the conclave itself. So they would speak during the congregations, in which elderly cardinals can take part, and provide a general outline—but not the full details—of their findings.

Wanted: New Evangelization and Vatican Reform

The leaks from the daily congregations confirmed what Vatican-watchers already knew: that the cardinals were concerned about evangelization, about resolving the sex-abuse scandal and the troubles of the Vatican bank, and about the infighting and inefficiency that had been exposed in the Roman Curia. Some prelates called for a thorough overhaul of the Vatican bureaucracy and the appointment of a chief of staff who would coordinate the work of the disparate agencies. The media dutifully reported these suggestions—although in a nod to the confidentiality of the discussions, the reports usually did not identify the cardinals who had made them.

The reporters, however, missed the most important address made during the general congregations, which came to light only after the conclave. A cardinal from Argentina, Jorge Bergoglio, captured the attention of his brothers with a short but strongly worded call for the Church to "come out of herself and go to the peripheries." When the Church does not do this, he said, "she becomes self-referential and then gets sick." This address evidently made many cardinals think of Bergoglio as a potential pope. It made such a deep impression on Havana's Cardinal Jaime Ortega that after

Bergoglio's election, he sought and received his permission to make the talk public.

Cardinal Bergoglio was by no means an unknown. According to the standard unauthorized account, in fact, he had been the runner-up to Cardinal Ratzinger in the conclave of 2005. But since that time he had been serving quietly as archbishop of Buenos Aires. Few saw him as a pope in waiting. He had not been touring the world and giving speeches. He had already submitted to the Holy See his resignation as archbishop, as required by canon law, upon reaching his seventy-fifth birthday. His name was not among the dozen mentioned by oddsmakers as the top candidates in 2013.

Yet at least a few cardinals remembered the support Bergoglio had received in the last conclave and believed that he would make a good candidate once again. Apparently Bergoglio himself was among them. In a chance meeting just before the conclave began, a young cleric playfully asked him what name he would take when he was elected. "Francis," came the prompt reply.

And so it was to be.

During the conclave itself, with the cardinals locked up in the Sistine Chapel, their deliberations sealed off from the outside world, the journalists assembled in Rome for the big story grew frustrated by the absence of material. One Fox News personality fumed that the Catholic Church obviously needed to change the way it chooses pontiffs. The current arrangement was not working—meaning that it was not providing him with anything to say.

Fortunately for the reporters, the result came quickly. On the second day of the conclave, on the fifth ballot, Cardinal Bergoglio was elected: the first Latin American and the first Jesuit to become the Roman pontiff. As soon as the white smoke rose from the chimney above the Sistine Chapel, a huge crowd assembled in St. Peter's Square to meet the new pope.

Several days later it emerged that immediately after his election, before his introduction to the public, the new pope had made it his top priority to call the pope emeritus, as Benedict XVI had decided to style himself. That turned out to be no easy task. When they entered the conclave, the cardinals had surrendered their cell phones, and the Sistine Chapel had been swept to ensure that there were no means of electronic communication. When the seal of the conclave was broken, the new pope scrambled through the apostolic palace looking for a working phone. He finally found one in a messy, crowded room that the Vatican Radio staff used for storage and put in the call to Castel Gandolfo. But the sequestered Benedict did not hear his phone ringing. He was watching television, waiting for the same news that the rest of the world wanted to hear.

The announcement, when it came, was confusing. Jean-Louis Tauran, who had the privilege as cardinal protodeacon to introduce the new pope to the world, drew a roar of applause when he uttered the traditional formula, "*Habemus papam!*" (We have a pope!) But the noise from the crowd and feedback from the public-address system obscured his words as he continued with the name: "*Eminentissimum ac reverendissimum Dominum, Dominum Georgium Marium, Sanctae Romanae Ecclesiae Cardinalem Bergoglio.*" Few people were expecting a "Georgium," and the murmurs from the square made it even more difficult to hear the "Bergoglio," so there was a moment of silence before the crowd—led by pilgrims from Argentina—began to applaud enthusiastically.

But as Cardinal Tauran continued, the excitement in St. Peter's Square increased. The new pope, he announced, had chosen the name "Francis." Evoking Francis of Assisi, one of the most beloved of all saints, the name indicated a commitment to simplicity, humility, and wholehearted love for all of God's creation. At the same time, it called to mind the message that the great saint had received from God in the church of San Damiano: "Francis, go, rebuild my house, which as you see is in ruins."

To grasp the full significance of this new pope's chosen name, consider that for 1,100 years, every newly elected pontiff had chosen a name that had been used by some other pope before him. The name of every pope since Lando, who reigned from 913 to 914, was followed by a Roman numeral, and the only pontiff to have chosen a new name, John Paul I, had explicitly named himself after his two immediate predecessors, John XXIII and Paul VI. So when he chose an entirely new name, Pope Francis indicated that he was prepared to strike out in a new direction.

A Sensational Debut

When the newly elected pope stepped out onto the loggia of the Vatican basilica, his appearance caused another sensation. He was dressed in the white papal cassock and zucchetto, but not in the mozzetta (a short scarlet cape) and stole that previous popes had worn for their first public appearance. After a somewhat awkward initial wave to the crowed, he stood quietly, his hands folded, until the applause began to die down. When he did speak, he began with the plainest of greetings: *Buona sera.*

Continuing in the same understated vein, the new pope told the crowd, "You know, it was the duty of the conclave to give Rome a new bishop." Well of course! No one in St. Peter's Square needed to be reminded of the business at hand. Francis went on: "It seems my brothers, the cardinals, have gone almost to the ends of the earth to find him. But here we are."

This was a sensation: a pope who told the world that the cardinals were obliged to choose *someone* as supreme pontiff and seemed almost apologetic for their selection. His words suggested that his election was happenstance—"here we are"—and he and the Catholic world would have to make the best of it.

As he continued, Francis referred to himself as the bishop of Rome, never speaking of himself as the "pope" and alluding to his new pre-eminence only indirectly, when he observed that the Church in Rome "is the one that leads all the churches in charity." Was this another display of humility? No doubt it was, but it was something more. Francis was laying the groundwork for a new understanding of the Petrine office, one that would drop the trappings of monarchical power and emphasize instead the role of the bishop of Rome as the focus of unity for the universal Church.

The new pope concluded with one more sensational gesture. He was expected to end his first address by giving his blessing *urbi et orbi*—to the city (here represented by the crowd in St. Peter's Square) and to the world. Francis introduced a new wrinkle: "Before the bishop blesses his people, I ask you to pray to the Lord to bless me." Then he, the "bishop," bowed his head, and a silence descended over the Vatican for several long moments before he finally gave his blessing. Even then he was not quite finished. "Pray for me," he urged the crowd, "and we will see one another soon."

After that first public appearance, Francis and all the cardinals who had elected him returned to the St. Martha's residence, where they had been lodged during the conclave, to collect their belongings. When the last minibus left St. Peter's Basilica, several cardinals were stunned to see that the successor of St. Peter was riding with them. He had not assumed that he could command his own vehicle and that Vatican aides would leap to do his bidding. He still thought of himself as one member—admittedly the leading member—of the college of bishops.

The next day, a Thursday, Francis slipped out of the Vatican to pray at the Roman basilica of St. Mary Major. Why did he choose that particular church? Because St. Mary Major is the oldest church in Rome dedicated to Our Lady, the largest and the most prominent? Yes, and the pope also chose it because the basilica houses the image of Mary *Salus Populi Romani*: the protector of the people of Rome. Again he was emphasizing the office of the bishop of Rome and his commitment to the local diocese.

The staff of the basilica was thrown into a frenzy by the unexpected visit. The building was, as usual, full of pilgrims and tourists. Should they be cleared out so that the pope could pray in private? Francis argued against any such special measures, insisting that he only wanted to pray before the beloved icon. In a compromise the staff did not empty the entire basilica, but cleared out the area where the pontiff would be.

On his return to the Vatican, the new pope stopped at the Domus Internationalis Paulus VI, where he had lodged before the conclave, to collect his luggage and settle his bill. Reports of this latest demonstration of papal humility—imagine a pontiff reaching into his own wallet to pay a bill!—flashed quickly around the world. Actually the scene was not unprecedented. After his election, Benedict XVI quietly visited the apartment he had occupied for years to pick up some books and other belongings, but no photographer recorded that pope's tending to his personal affairs.

The image of the new pope as a simple, humble man shunning the pretentious trappings of the papal court was quickly fixed in the public's mind. But there was one sour note, mostly lost in the adulatory media coverage of the new pontificate. According to some reporters, when an aide tried to place the traditional mozzetta across his shoulders before his first appearance on the loggia of St. Peter's, Francis brushed him away testily, declaring that "the carnival is over."

The reports seemed improbable. The reference to the "carnival," if true, was obviously a slap at Pope Benedict, who had gladly revived the use of some traditional papal vestments, such as the broad-brimmed saturno and the red slippers, because of his keen appreciation for the history and authority they symbolized. Why would a new pope, at this moment before a triumphant appearance, make an acerbic remark about his predecessor? Another account had the pope declining the mozzetta with a gentle "I would prefer not to." But why would a reporter invent the "carnival" comment if it had not been made? And if he really had used that word, or something like it, why was the newly elected pope so angry?

CHAPTER TWO

The Francis Effect

During the early days of his pontificate, Pope Francis captured the world's attention with his unconventional style. His plain speech and his disdain for pomp conflicted with stereotypical views about how a pope should speak and act. Some were delighted by his egalitarian approach, while others—particularly lovers of Vatican traditions—were dismayed. But everyone was paying attention.

St. Peter's Square was packed for the pope's first public audience on Sunday, March 17, 2013. He greeted the enormous crowd simply, in the same way that he had introduced himself after his election: *Buon giorno!* Speaking in Italian and peppering his remarks with light-hearted digressions, he earned appreciative applause. Then after about fifteen minutes he brought the midday address to a cheery conclusion: "Have a good day, and enjoy your lunch."

After touring the papal apartments, Francis decided that he could not live in the grand isolation of the apostolic palace and moved permanently into the Domus Sanctae Marthae—St. Martha's House—the Vatican guesthouse where he and the other cardinals had lodged during the conclave. There he would enjoy the constant stream of visitors to Rome along with the steady traffic of Vatican officials.

Next the pope began to celebrate Mass each morning in the chapel of the St. Martha's residence with a congregation composed of whoever happened to be staying there at the time. Here too he was breaking new ground, as his predecessors had celebrated daily Mass privately or with a few invited guests in a chapel in the apostolic palace. He preached every day—without the miter that symbolized his pontifical rank—and brief reports on those short homilies were provided daily by Vatican Radio.

Francis was predictably unpredictable. He placed his own phone calls, shocking those who received an unscheduled call from the Roman pontiff. Soon after his election he called the proprietor of the newsstand in Buenos Aires where he had picked up his newspaper each morning to cancel his subscription—and to chat a bit. He popped up unexpectedly in shops across Rome, first to buy new eyeglasses, then for a pair of orthopedic shoes.

Reporters loved this new pope who provided them with an endless supply of interesting stories, and he received overwhelmingly favorable media coverage. Speaking with a reporter in Rome who had been covering the Vatican for some years, I remarked on the sympathetic treatment that Francis received from the press. My journalist friend emphatically agreed, noting that reporters—including some who were not particularly enamored of the pope—were leaving some potentially damaging stories unreported because they thought no one wanted to hear bad news about this pontiff. "I can't imagine what it would take" to turn the media against Francis, he said.

A case in point is the media's lack of interest, after a short flurry of attention, in the charge that Father Bergoglio, while a Jesuit provincial, had supported Argentina's military dictatorship in the 1970s. A left-wing Argentine journalist, Horatio Verbitsky, accused Bergoglio of complicity in the arrest of two radical Jesuit priests who were under his charge. Verbitsky offered little evidence for his claim apart from suspicions voiced by one of the priests in question. That priest was deceased by the time Bergoglio became pope, and the other expressed confidence that Bergoglio had not been involved. But reporters have been known to probe into such a story on the slim chance that they might uncover a sensational scandal. (To this day, some writers make a point of mentioning that Benedict XVI was a member of a Nazi youth group—not bothering to note that the young Ratzinger was compelled to join, and eventually walked away from the group without permission, risking arrest for desertion.) While there was scant evidence, moreover, that Bergoglio was responsible for the imprisonment of these two Jesuits, there was still ample room for questions about the future pope's relationship with the military government. Those questions were not raised, and the media quickly dropped the story.

The media focused instead on the messages that the pope was delivering, often in striking, earthy language. He encouraged young people to "shake things up" and "make a mess." He said that good bishops, like good shepherds, should have "the smell of their sheep." He lamented that some Catholics had become "obsessed" with public issues such as abortion, when they should be spending their energies on the more important task of drawing people closer to Christ. He spoke—with a frequency that some people found alarming—about the devil. He likened the Church to a field hospital, caring for the wounded. In marked contrast to the careful, scholarly Benedict XVI, Francis spoke impulsively; he often seemed to be provoking his audiences deliberately.

With the pope constantly in the headlines, Catholics and non-Catholics alike found themselves talking more frequently about the Catholic Church. Italian priests reported longer lines of people coming to confession, including many who had been away from the sacrament for years. American clerics said they noticed the same trend. The excitement surrounding the pontiff seemed to encourage people to practice their faith in simple, direct ways. Journalists dubbed this the "Francis effect," and the pope's most enthusiastic supporters predicted a bull market for conversions to the Catholic Faith.

"Who Am I to Judge?"

But the "Francis effect" came at a cost. If the pope's brash statements were sometimes inspiring, they were also sometimes confusing, and if he aimed to provoke, he occasionally offended. As time passed, the pope's support for controversial causes and his penchant for ad-lib statements began to raise eyebrows, then to prompt concerns.

At first, Francis seemed to defy easy classification as a "liberal" or "conservative," but as the months passed, a pattern emerged of support for causes usually associated with the political Left—environmentalism, disarmament, unrestricted immigration, income redistribution. His warning about being "obsessed" with abortion and contraception made many loyal Catholics uneasy; it hardly seemed necessary to complain about an "obsession" with issues that are rarely even mentioned in a typical parish. Still, even a stalwart pro-life Catholic could swallow hard and accept the pope's admonition, reading it as a call for a new rhetorical strategy or for recognizing that evangelization is more important than political activism.

After all, on other hot-button political issues, Francis seemed to have taken a conservative position—at least initially. During his tenure as archbishop of Buenos Aires he had denounced a proposal for acceptance of same-sex marriage as the work of the devil. More recently, he had admitted that he was concerned about the possible influence of a "gay lobby" within the Vatican.

But if orthodox Catholics had concluded that Francis would stand firm against homosexual influence within the Church, their confidence was shattered by his remarks to reporters on a trip to Brazil in July 2013. Asked about homosexual priests, he replied, "If they accept the Lord and have good will, who am I to judge them?"

The context of that statement is important. Sandro Magister, an influential Vatican reporter for the Italian journal *L'Espresso*, had reported that Msgr. Battista Ricca, whom Francis had recently appointed prelate of the Vatican bank, had a history of scandalous homosexual affairs. Magister went on to charge that the Vatican's "gay lobby" had whitewashed Msgr. Ricca's record to smooth the way for his appointment. Francis insisted that he had looked into the charges and satisfied himself that "there was nothing there."

Having answered the reporter's question, the pope might have stopped there, but he continued, apparently wanting to say something about homosexuality. Although there had been many reports about a "gay lobby" at the Vatican, there was no clearly identifiable group—he had "never seen it on a Vatican ID card," he joked. It is important, he said, to distinguish between priests who might have a homosexual orientation and those who might be active in a "lobby" within the Church. "The problem isn't the orientation," he concluded; "the problem is having a lobby."

Yes, but the pope's remarks did not address the existing Vatican policy, set forth in 2005 in an instruction from the Congregation for Catholic Education, that men with homosexual tendencies should not be ordained to the priesthood. Nor did they ease concerns about the influence of homosexual priests in Rome and elsewhere. More important still, the key words in his reply to the question—the "sound bite" that would be carried around the world and repeated for years—were "Who am I to judge?" As reported by journalists generally favorable to the homosexual cause, the pope's statement seemed to suggest that the Church should move away from its clear and constant teaching that homosexual acts are gravely immoral. And who is the world's foremost defender of the Church's constant teaching? The bishop of Rome. Insofar as he was raising questions about the authority of Church teaching, Francis was undercutting his own authority as pontiff. The political philosopher Hannah Arendt argued that an active conscience sometimes requires a person to judge the actions of others. As she wrote in her personal notes, "If you say to yourself in such matters: who am I to judge?—you are already lost."

The pope's statement caused an immediate uproar, as gay activists rushed to claim the pontiff as their ally and editorial writers welcomed what they saw as a more enlightened Catholic position. Orthodox Catholics strove valiantly to limit the damage, pointing out that the pope was speaking extemporaneously, that he was not making an authoritative statement, and that in any case he had not contradicted any aspect of Church teaching. Yet the pope *had* made the fateful statement—"Who am I to judge?"—and the Catholic world would be forced to live with its legacy.

Why did Francis allow himself to address such a controversial topic without preparing his answer carefully? Why were the most famous words of his pontificate uttered in an informal question-and-answer session on an airplane ride?

The Pope's Favorite Interviewer

"Interviews are not my forte," Cardinal Jorge Bergoglio once remarked to reporters in Buenos Aires. For that reason he seldom sat down to speak with journalists on the record. When two reporters sought a lengthy formal interview, he declined their request and encouraged them instead to publish excerpts from his sermons and essays. But now, as Roman pontiff, when his word carries far more weight, he grants interviews frequently—often with damaging results.

In October 2013, for example, the pope sat down with the journalist Eugenio Scalfari, an avowed atheist. Their exchange, published in, *La Repubblica*, a left-leaning newspaper Scalfari co-founded, contained a series of bombshells. The pope dismissed proselytism as "solemn non-sense," called the Vatican court "the leprosy of the papacy," and proclaimed, "The most serious of the evils that afflict the world these days are youth unemployment and the loneliness of the old." Commenting on the pope's ideas, Scalfari wrote: "If the Church becomes more like him and becomes what he wants it to be, it will be an epochal change."

After the interview was published—catching the Vatican's public relations staff entirely by surprise, since they had not been informed about it—some shocking details emerged. Scalfari, who was ninety years old at the time, had not recorded the pope's answers to his questions or even taken notes but had relied on his memory to reconstruct the pope's words. The accuracy of the quotations attributed to the pontiff in *La Repubblica* was therefore questionable. No competent public relations adviser would have allowed his client to be caught in such a dangerous situation. But Francis had not asked for advice before granting the interview.

Incredibly, the pope then submitted to *another* interview with Scalfari in July 2014, and again the elderly journalist relied on his memory for the quotations. Making no claim to a photographic memory, Scalfari explained that he preferred to put the thoughts of his subject (in this case Pope Francis) into his own, presumably more elegant, words. That approach might be justified if Scalfari understood perfectly what his subject was saying, but no one understands another man perfectly. Scalfari's reconstructed quotations, then, reflected what Scalfari understood the pope to be saying, which might have been quite different from what the pope intended.

Sure enough, the interview again contained some dynamite. Francis was quoted as saying that there were priests, and "even bishops and cardinals," guilty of pedophilia. "And others, more numerous, know but keep silent," he added. The Vatican press office found it necessary to issue a warning that the quotations attributed to the pope were not reliable. Father Federico Lombardi, the papal spokesman, compounded the problem by remarking that the pope's exchange with Scalfari had been "very cordial and most interesting" and that the "overall theme of the article captures the spirit of the conversation." So helpless readers were left to guess for themselves which passages, if any, were inaccurate.

In March 2015, the talkative pope again spoke with Scalfari for *La Repubblica*. This time Francis—at least as interpreted by his favorite interviewer—appeared to cast doubt on the existence of hell:

> What happens to that lost soul? Will it be punished? And how? The response of Francis is distinct and clear: there is no punishment, but the annihilation of that soul. All the

others will participate in the beatitude of living in the presence of the Father. The souls that are annihilated will not take part in that banquet; with the death of the body their journey is finished.

The First Encyclical

Almost lost in the blizzard of interviews, homilies, and off-the-cuff statements, were the pope's first few formal teaching documents. His first encyclical, *Lumen Fidei* ("The Light of Faith"), published in June 2013, relatively soon after his installation, was begun by Benedict XVI as the third of a trio of encyclicals on the theological virtues of charity, hope, and faith. Francis grafted his own ideas onto the draft that Benedict had left him, the result being an odd hybrid document.

In its completed form, *Lumen Fidei* is definitely the work of Francis, not Benedict. An encyclical is a teaching document, carrying the authority of the Roman pontiff. Benedict had relinquished that authority. Francis was free to do whatever he wanted with the manuscript that Benedict left him—discard it, amend it, or complete it—and it became *his* encyclical. Still, astute readers can detect traces of Benedict's prose style and even identify which sections of the document were prepared by which pontiff.

At the press conference introducing the new encyclical, Archbishop Rino Fisichella, the president of the Pontifical Council for the Promotion of the New Evangelization, commented on the question of authorship: "It must be said without hesitation that while *Lumen fidei* resumes some of the intuition and themes typical of the ministry of Benedict XVI, it is fully Pope Francis's text." Francis himself, clearly intent on underlining that his teachings are in full accord with those of Benedict, observes in his introduction that the text is "in continuity with all that the Church's magisterium has pronounced on this theological virtue."

The encyclical does cover some of the arguments that were central to the teaching of Benedict XVI during his pontificate, such as the importance of joining faith and reason and the danger of eliminating God from public discussion. The document also has the scholarly tone of the pope emeritus, including allusions to Nietzsche, Dante, Dostoevsky, Wittgenstein, and T. S. Eliot, along with citations from Church Fathers and a plethora of Scriptural references. At the same time, the encyclical covers themes that Francis has emphasized, including the impossibility of achieving justification through one's own merits and the need to put faith into action through help for the poor.

Lumen Fidei opens with the observation that the gift of faith has always been associated with light, which enables believers to see things clearly. In modern thought, however, "faith came to be associated with darkness," and philosophers sought for truth divorced from faith. That quest proved illusory, the pope writes: "Slowly but surely, however, it would become evident that the light of autonomous reason is not enough to illumine the future; ultimately the future remains shadowy and fraught with fear of the unknown." The encyclical insists on the need to regain a proper understanding of the natural partnership between faith and reason. "Today more than ever, we need to be reminded of this bond between faith and truth, given the crisis of truth in our age."

"Anyone who sets off on the path of doing good to others," writes Francis, "is already drawing near to God, is already sustained by his help, for it is characteristic of the divine light to brighten our eyes whenever we walk towards the fullness of love." Nevertheless, he writes, "It is impossible to believe on our own." In the New Covenant, Jesus offers the Church as the guarantor of faith. Moreover, the Faith is transmitted and strengthened through the sacramental life of the Church, especially in baptism. Sharing in the Faith, all members of the Church, at all times, "possess a unity which enriches us because it is given to us and makes us one."

A Blueprint for the Papacy?

The next major document by Francis was also a hybrid, but in a different sense. *Evangelii Gaudium* ("The Joy of the Gospel"), made public in November 2013, is an apostolic exhortation—a papal document responding to a meeting of the Synod of Bishops. The synod had met in October 2012, during the pontificate of Benedict XVI, to consider the "new evangelization." But Benedict had not drafted a response, and Francis, inheriting the recommendations that the bishops had reached, said he wanted to place them in a broader framework.

The result was, unfortunately, a very long document. No doubt the pontiff began with a summary of the themes that arose in the synod discussions and did his best to incorporate them all, but he occasionally strayed from his main focus or circled back to subjects that he had already discussed. The sheer length of the text (222 pages, in the version released by the Vatican) would discourage many readers.

Nevertheless, readers who took the time to read this apostolic exhortation—or even the opening passages, which provide a good sense of the pope's overall message—were rewarded. Francis writes with great energy, and the text is liberally sprinkled with highly quotable passages. (It is safe to say, I think, that this is the first papal document in which the official English translation contains the word "sourpusses.")

In *Evangelii Gaudium*, Francis offers not only a guide to the "new evangelization" but also an outline of his plans for Church reform. In other words, the document is a blueprint for his pontificate.

Evangelization, the pope insists, is the very essence of the Church's mission. The drive to share the Good News of the Gospel is fueled—as the exhortation's opening words suggest—by the joy that believers find in their faith. Today, the Church must convey that joy to a troubled world. Francis calls for a new sense of urgency and paring down bureaucratic structures and attitudes. In a sentence that encapsulates his approach to reform, he writes: "Pastoral ministry in a missionary key seeks to abandon the complacent attitude that says: 'We have always done it this way.'"

Father Roger Landry, a pastor and gifted preacher from Massachusetts, captured the message nicely: "Pope Francis says that the fundamental reform the Church needs is from one of self-preservation of Church structures to a permanent state of mission."

"There are ecclesial structures which can hamper efforts at evangelization," Francis writes, "yet even good structures are only helpful when there is a life constantly driving, sustaining and assessing them." He expresses his determination to streamline the organization of the Church to stimulate, rather than retard, apostolic activity.

Outlining his plans for reform, the pope recognizes the need to decentralize. The Vatican, he insists, is there to help diocesan bishops, not to control them, and he proposes a greater role for episcopal conferences so they can stimulate efforts at the national level rather than always looking to Rome. "Excessive centralization, rather than proving helpful, complicates the Church's life and missionary outreach," the pope writes.

The papacy itself should be reformed, Francis continues, for the sake of Christian unity. Citing the desire of John Paul II to find a way of exercising the Petrine ministry that would preserve papal primacy while allowing full scope for the authority of diocesan bishops, he laments, "We have made little progress in this regard."

The bulk of *Evangelii Gaudium* is devoted to the challenge of evangelization. Francis provides a rich variety of useful suggestions for pastors and for lay people who wish to share their faith. In the most detailed, practical section, he focuses at length—"somewhat meticulously," as he puts it—on how priests should prepare their homilies.

At the same time, the pope is scornful of efforts to "circle the wagons" and preserve the institutional prestige of the Church. He is critical of any Catholic who "would rather be the general of a defeated army than a mere private in a unit which continues to fight."

In this long document, Francis discourses at some length about economic affairs, challenging the faithful to recognize that the pursuit of wealth is not the purpose of life. He is particularly critical of the global economic system, which he says is founded on the idolatrous worship of material success. That message drew angry responses from defenders of free-market economic systems, who complained that the pope had ignored the successes of capitalism and implicitly endorsed socialism.

Bishop James Conley of Lincoln, Nebraska—from whom one would expect sympathy for the free-market theorists—dismissed those criticisms as "a sophomoric caricature" of the papal document, which follows a well-worn path of Catholic social teaching. As he wrote in the conservative journal *National Review*,

> *Evangelii Gaudium* did not reject capitalism, or even particular market theories. Instead, it rejected idolatry of any economic system as a panacea, and it called Catholics to human solidarity in the context of public policy. The Pope affirmed that markets must be understood and administered in justice, with due regard for the sovereignty and solidarity of families and human dignity. Pope Benedict XVI presented similar ideas in depth in 2009, as did Saint Thomas Aquinas and Saint Augustine.

The Environmentalist Encyclical

Lumen Fidei was not a controversial document, and while *Evangelii Gaudium* made some conservative readers uneasy, others insisted that the pope was not straying into partisan politics. With his second encyclical, however, Francis turned to a topic with obvious political implications: the environment.

Laudato Si', bearing the subtitle *On Care for Our Common Home*, was leaked to the media in advance of the official publication in June 2015, and journalists quickly announced that it was devoted to the topic of "climate change." That assessment was not quite accurate—any more than it would be accurate to say that Shakespeare's *Romeo and Juliet* is a play about suicide. Yes, the topic is mentioned; indeed it is a very important part of the story. But it is not the main theme.

A reader disengaged from today's ideological battles, having digested the full 192-page text, might conclude that the encyclical is mostly about sustainable development, or anthropocentrism, or the unequal profits and burdens associated with exploitation of natural resources. More generally it is about living in harmony with nature, preserving a humble reverence for the intricate beauty and balance of creation. One perceptive reader remarked, quite accurately, that *Laudato Si'* could be read as this pope's homage to his two most recent predecessors, whose thoughts are cited constantly.

It could be argued that the most interesting facet of the encyclical is the pope's development of the concept of "ecological debt." Previous Roman pontiffs had referred to the "social mortgage" on private property. "Ecological debt" is a similar concept. In Catholic social teaching, the right to private property is essential, but it is not absolute. Since all material resources should serve the common good, and since anyone in possession of valuable property is ultimately indebted to God for his blessings, the wealthy few have a moral obligation to use their resources in ways that serve the poor. The "social mortgage," then, is roughly equivalent to *noblesse oblige*—with money and power come certain implied obligations to the community. The concept of "ecological debt" is based on the same logic. When we extract ore or fossil fuels from the earth or put dangerous chemicals into the air and water, we are leaving problems for our children and grandchildren. We should stop running up environmental debts that future generations must repay or at least, Francis argues, find ways to help them pay down those debts.

Many analysts had predicted that the pope would denounce climate-change skepticism. They were not disappointed. "A very solid scientific consensus indicates that we are presently witnessing a disturbing warming of the climatic system," Francis writes, noting that "a number of scientific studies indicate that most global warming in recent decades is due to the great concentration of greenhouse gases (carbon dioxide, methane, nitrogen oxides and others) released mainly as a result of human activity."

A spiritual leader weighing in on a scientific debate, Francis is obviously out of his element. Man-made climate change either is or is not a scientific reality. A pronouncement by the pope—who has no special authority on scientific issues—will not affect that reality one way or another. In *Laudato Si'*, the pontiff sides with the majority opinion, and he does so unnecessarily, because the question of climate change is not central to the moral argument that he is exploring.[1]

Plunging deeper into the scientific and political debate, Francis goes on to declare that nature "now cries out to us because of the harm we have inflicted on her by our irresponsible use and abuse of the goods with which God has endowed her." Just as Pope John XXIII had issued his encyclical *Pacem in Terris* when mankind stood on the brink of nuclear disaster, Francis declares, so he is issuing *Laudato Si'* at a time of looming environmental disaster.

The pope's "green" sympathies are evident throughout the document. In his laments over the loss of natural scenery and of family farms, powerful multinational corporations, and blighted urban landscapes, Francis can be read as a conventional liberal. But the same complaints are characteristic of an important strain of conservatism, represented by the agrarians and the distributists, the followers of Russell Kirk and the small-is-beautiful disciples of E. F. Schumacher. Readers from both ends of the political spectrum could find in this document some reasons to cheer.

Take, for instance (although it is definitely not a minor issue), the pope's insistence on reverence for all human life. It is "troubling,"

---

1 Bishop Marcelo Sánchez Sorondo, the chancellor of the Pontifical Academy of Sciences, confused matters in December 2015 by stating at a conference that the pope's judgment on climate change "must be considered magisterium [that is, official Church teaching]—it is not an opinion." The American Jesuit Joseph Fessio corrected that error in an interview with LifeSite News: "Neither the pope nor Bishop Sorondo can speak on a matter of science with any binding authority, so to use the word 'magisterium' in both cases is equivocal at best, and ignorant in any case. To equate a papal position on abortion with a position on global warming [as Bishop Sorondo had done] is worse than wrong; it is an embarrassment for the Church."

he writes, "that, when some ecological movements defend the integrity of the environment, rightly demanding that certain limits be imposed on scientific research, they sometimes fail to apply those same principles to human life." And he warns of a "constant schizophrenia, wherein a technocracy which sees no intrinsic value in lesser beings coexists with the other extreme, which sees no special value in human beings." The argument that population growth is the source of our environmental woes is, he said "one way of refusing to face the issues."

On the other hand, defenders of free-market economics were once again rattled by the pope's argument that reliance on the market alone is a form of moral relativism. Later he adds: "To claim economic freedom while real conditions bar many people from actual access to it, and while possibilities for employment continue to shrink, is to practice a doublespeak which brings politics into disrepute."

Above all the pope criticizes a society that defines progress in terms of the stimulation and satisfaction of purely material needs: "This paradigm leads people to believe that they are free as long as they have the supposed freedom to consume." Issuing a challenge to the economic profession, the pontiff writes, "The principle of the maximization of profits, frequently isolated from other considerations, reflects a misunderstanding of the very concept of the economy."

But wait—if the goal of economic activity is not to maximize profits, what *is* the goal? Francis suggests a broader conception of what constitutes success. Again and again he speaks of "sustainable development," emphasizing that the economic activities of a healthy society should pave the way for further "sustainable development" in future generations.

The characteristically Christian instinct to share—both with the poor and with future generations—is diametrically opposed to the impulses of what Francis condemns as a "throwaway culture." In *Laudato Si'* the pontiff expands on this theme, decrying the tendency of modern man to identify productive resources, use them up, and move on without a thought to the long-term consequences. The poor do not enjoy the same opportunities to profit from the results of technological progress, the pope contends, yet they suffer disproportionately from the environmental harm. Care for the environment, therefore, is a form of care for the poor.

A Climate-Reform Rally in St. Peter's Square

If this encyclical furnished the argument for Catholic environmental activism, the Vatican followed up with a concrete—and distinctly partisan—application of that argument a few months later. In December 2015, a light show billed as "Fiat Lux: Illuminating Our Common Home" was displayed across the façade of St. Peter's Basilica. Archbishop Fisichella said that the show, "inspired by the most recent encyclical of Pope Francis, *Laudato si'*, is intended to present the beauty of creation, especially on the occasion of the Twenty-first United Nations Climate Change Conference." The show's promoters also produced a Fiat Lux website, which encouraged visitors to "demand climate reform" and urged them to sign a petition addressed to "President Obama and the leaders of China, European Union, India and Russia," who "represent the world's five largest carbon emitters" and "therefore hold the future of countless species in [their] hands."

"Fiat Lux," a purely secular affair, was produced by foundations engaged in partisan political activity, with the backing of some of the world's wealthiest men, including Paul Allen, the co-founder of Microsoft, and Li Ka Shing, a Hong Kong magnate believed to be the richest man in Asia. If the show, an impressive technical achievement, had been displayed in a secular setting—the wall of the Grand Canyon, for example, or the white cliffs of Dover—few would have objected. Then again, few would have noticed. The show drew worldwide attention precisely because it was displayed on the most famous church in the world, a universally recognized symbol of the Catholic Faith. The purpose of the light show was to put environmentalism in the foreground with the Catholic Faith as a backdrop, to enlist religious support without supporting religion.

The sophisticated foundation executives who suborned the Vatican to arrange this show knew exactly what they were doing. Did the Vatican, under Francis, recognize how the influence of the Church was being exploited? Any Christian—any deist, for that matter—should recognize the moral obligation to be a good steward of creation. If hot-button political debates have predisposed some of us to be leery of environmentalist rhetoric, all the more reason for a Roman pontiff to seek a different perspective, one more consistent with the Faith.

The pope's environmental advocacy veered into doctrinal territory in his message for the World Day of Prayer for Creation in September 2016, when he said that care for the environment should be added to the Church's traditional list of the corporal and spiritual works of mercy. Unlike his questionable judgments on scientific and political issues, his remarks about the works of mercy pertain directly to the moral teachings of the Church.

Unless his statement is to be dismissed as a rhetorical flourish, the pope was suggesting an alteration in the Catechism. Young Catholics of future generations would be taught that there are *eight* works in each category. Alongside corporal works like feeding the hungry and clothing the naked, they would find care for the environment. Alongside spiritual works like instructing the ignorant and admonishing sinners, they would find…what, exactly? Support for the Sierra Club? That change cannot easily be undone.

Francis was not proposing an organic change to the list of works of mercy. He was putting things—virtuous actions, perhaps—in a category where they did not belong. Turning off unnecessary lights, as the pope urges, is undoubtedly a good idea. But it is *not* a work of mercy as Catholics have always understood that term. The traditional works of mercy—corporal and spiritual—all have a human person as both subject and object. The object is a person in some kind of need. The subject is you or I—a person challenged to imitate Christ by filling that need. In the new works of mercy that Francis proposed, the object is the natural environment, not a human soul. And many people will assume that the subject of these new works is not the individual Christian but the government, which should make laws to protect the environment.

Exhorting the faithful to turn off lights, join car pools, and separate paper from plastics—however commendable such acts may be—dilutes the authority of the pope's teaching office, inviting the danger that his condemnations of blasphemy and abortion will be taken as the same sort of "nice" suggestions as his call for car pools.

Explaining Away the Pope's Statements

The pope's statements on environmental affairs required an assessment of scientific evidence that he is not qualified to make. The same criticism could be leveled at many of his comments on economic affairs.

In March 2017, Francis publicly recognized a group of executives from the Sky Italy television network who were in attendance at his weekly general audience. Sky Italy had recently announced plans to downsize and restructure, and three hundred workers would be asked to move from Rome to Milan. Addressing these executives, the pontiff said, "He who shuts factories and closes companies as a result of economic operations and unclear negotiations, depriving men and women from work, commits a very grave sin." Admittedly, the remarks were muddled. (Translators could not be blamed for the confusion; the sentence is equally unclear in the Italian.) But in the context of addressing representatives of a specific corporation, the pope appears to accuse the executives of Sky Italy of "a very grave sin." Did he understand the circumstances that had prompted the corporate decision? When he said that layoffs should never be caused by "economic operations," what on earth did he mean? If employers are forbidden to close plants, must they leave the plants open even when they are losing money, until the corporation runs into bankruptcy—and the employees lose their positions anyway?

With such imprudent statements, Francis left loyal Catholics grasping for ways to interpret his message so that they could maintain the wholehearted support they had always given to the Roman pontiff. As the months of the pontificate passed, and the ledger of partisan messages grew steadily more unbalanced, that effort became more and more difficult.

From the start the pope's unconventional approach has dismayed some Catholics. Soon after his election, he visited the Vatican press office to introduce himself to the reporters who cover the Holy See. The journalists expected him to conclude the visit with a blessing. But the new pope decided not to make the sign of the Cross, telling them, "Since many of you do not belong to the Catholic Church, and others are not believers, I will cordially impart this blessing to each of you in silence, with respect for the conscience of each individual, but in the knowledge that each one of you is a child of God." Then he bowed his head, prayed in silence for a few moments, and left the room. Puzzled Catholic journalists—and the vast majority of Vatican journalists are Catholic—looked confusedly at each other, feeling as if the event had not quite ended. One reporter told me that he felt he had been cheated out of a papal blessing.

Similarly, when he spoke at the White House and before a joint session of Congress in September 2015, Francis never mentioned the name of Jesus Christ. His defenders explained that it would be inappropriate to mention the Lord's name in a formal address to a secular audience. But when St. Peter was admonished "not to teach in this name" (Acts: 5:28), he ignored the restriction. Why should his successor act differently now? In his appearance before Congress the pope was treated as a secular head of state and clumsily introduced to the assembly with the nonsensical title "the Pope of the Holy See." But why should American politicians be interested in the opinions of the leader of a tiny city-state? When the bishop of Rome travels abroad, he might explain why people should listen to his message: because he speaks in the name of Jesus.

In the early months of the papacy it was possible to explain the pope's more troublesome statements as part of an effort to strike a balance between liberal and conservative views. In November 2013, Ross Douthat, a columnist for the *New York Times* and a Catholic, suggested that the pontiff was trying to end "a kind of low-grade institutional civil war" that had afflicted the Church since the Second Vatican Council and had "ultimately left everyone a loser." I myself wrote that analysts on both ends of the political and theological spectrums were, for their own partisan purposes, trying to portray the pope as a radical. A year later, I was ready to conclude that maybe Francis really *was* a radical, and Douthat was several strides ahead of me, suggesting that orthodox Catholics "might want to consider the possibility that they have a role to play, and that this Pope may be preserved from error only if the Church itself resists him."

Sandro Magister wrote in March 2015 that Francis was doing a "two-step," mixing statements of traditional Catholic teaching with surprising concessions to liberal secular thinking. "The novelty of his pontificate," he wrote, "is that along with these reaffirmations of perennial doctrine it also gives free rein to doctrines and pastoral practices of a different and sometimes opposite nature."

Mixed Messages on Contraception ...

In January 2015, Francis drew headlines with another of his famous airborne interviews. En route to the Philippines, he revealed to reporters that he had once "rebuked" a woman with a history of troubled pregnancies who was expecting her eighth child, asking her, "But do you want to leave seven orphans?" He called for "responsible parenthood." The pope did not endorse artificial contraception and was careful to state that "God gives you methods to be responsible," alluding to natural family planning. But his remarks provoked a fresh round of editorial mockery of Catholics for their rejection of birth control—mockery in which the pontiff himself seemed to join with his comment, "Some think that, excuse me if I use that word, that in order to be good Catholics we have to be like rabbits. No!"

Again, a pattern of statements that was confusing in 2015 began to seem clear a year later. In February 2016, in another airplane interview—the same interview in which he suggested that a wall-building Donald Trump was "not Christian"—the pope responded to a question about a UN proposal to distribute contraceptives in parts of Latin America affected by the Zika virus, which can cause serious birth defects. "Avoiding pregnancy is not an absolute evil," Francis replied.

Asked whether contraception is the "lesser of two evils" when the Zika virus threatens birth defects, the pope replied in part, "On the lesser evil, avoiding pregnancy, we are speaking in terms of a conflict between the Fifth and Sixth Commandments." What conflict? Did he mean to suggest that in some cases, adhering to one of God's laws might entail violating another?

In the next sentence, the pope referred to a purported decision by Pope Paul VI authorizing nuns in the Belgian Congo to use contraceptives when they were threatened with rape. But it is not entirely clear what direction Paul VI actually gave to the nuns. If he did authorize the use of contraceptives, some Catholic moral theologians argue, his advice was unwise. In any event, that papal directive did not apply to the situation in Zika-stricken Latin America. Contraception is immoral because it violates the integrity of the marital act. In the Congo, some moral theologians argued, contraception was justified as a means of thwarting an act of violence—logic that would not apply to the Zika case.

True, the pope did not actually *say* that contraception could be justified. He simply said that "avoiding pregnancy is not an absolute evil." But what other conclusion were reporters likely to draw from his statement? If you ask me whether it is justifiable to rob a bank, and I reply that bank robbery is not an absolute evil, haven't I indicated that

I am open to a discussion about whether bank robbery is licit in certain circumstances? Certainly I have *not* given the impression that I think bank robbery is always immoral.

UN officials were suggesting that married couples should routinely practice artificial contraception because of the Zika epidemic. Nothing in the pope's remarks suggested that there was a moral problem with that approach. Moreover the pope failed to point out the flaw in the major premise of the argument for routine contraception: the *assumption* that the Zika virus was responsible for microcephaly. But there was little scientific evidence to support that assumption, as the pope's own representative highlighted in a presentation to the United Nations.

How damaging was this papal interview? Loyal defenders of the pontiff said that his words had been taken out of context. But the problem was not sensationalistic reporting. Proponents of contraception and abortion had been exploiting the Zika epidemic to advance their cause. In his confusing statement, Francis had conveyed the impression that he was ready to discuss the morality of contraception in the context of the Zika epidemic.

... And on Gender Ideology

Later in 2016, the pope caused dismay with his statement on another hot topic: gender ideology. During an October visit to Tbilisi, Georgia, the pontiff had denounced gender ideology in ringing terms. "Today there is a world war to destroy marriage," he said, and gender theory is an important part of it. He urged the people of Georgia to resist such "ideological colonizations which destroy—not with weapons but with ideas." Strong words, these.

But the very next day, in an illustration of what Sandro Magister had called the "two-step," the pope undercut his own statement. In an exchange with reporters on his flight back to Rome—another airplane interview!—he showed himself willing to give gender theorists what they want most: the freedom to change pronouns.

In answer to an American journalist's question about his condemnation of gender theory, the pope delivered a convoluted yet revealing reply:

> Last year I received a letter from a Spaniard who told me his story as a child, a young man, he was a girl, a girl who suffered so much because he felt like a boy, but was physically a girl. He told his mother and the mom … [the girl] was around 22 years old said that she would like to do the surgical intervention and all of those things. And the mother said not to do it while she was still alive. She was elderly and she died soon after. She had the surgery and an employee of a ministry in the city of Spain went to the bishop, who accompanied [this person] a lot. Good bishop. I spent time accompanying this man. Then [the man] got married, he changed his civil identity, got married and wrote me a letter saying that for him it would be a consolation to come with his wife, he who was she, but him!

Notice that last line: the pope's reference to "he who was she, but him!" Those words were not included in the Vatican's official summary of the interview, but the telling phrase was reported by other news agencies, with only small variations in the translations. The pope said that a "she" had become a "he." Even according to the official Vatican summary, he introduced the individual, born female, as "a Spanish man." He accepted the change of sexual identity as a fact.

The pope went on to say that he had met with the Spanish couple, "and they were very happy." Nowhere did he suggest that the "he who was she" was troubled or had done anything wrong. Indeed, the pope's full response to the reporter's question suggested only that it was wrong to teach gender ideology in schools, "to change the mentality" of students. In this case, the Spanish girl apparently made her own decision to manipulate her sexual identity, and the pontiff registered no objection. He applauded the Spanish prelate who "accompanied him greatly." Did that bishop urge the girl not to disfigure herself, not to rebel against God's plan for her life? If he did, Francis did not mention it.

A young girl who is unhappy as a girl needs sympathy, support, and loving care. But if she thinks of herself as a boy, she should not be encouraged in that delusion. A girl is a girl, and a boy is a boy, and neither medical procedures nor hormone injections can change that reality. When God established the human race, the book of Genesis tells us, "male and female he created them." The distinction between male and female identity is the great "given," an integral part of God's plan—not just for humanity as a whole but for each one of us. The notion that one can decide one's own sex entails a rejection of creation. It is a claim that the individual can build his own reality, that there are no "givens"—in short a rejection of God's sovereignty.

So what happened in the case of that unfortunate Spanish girl? Did God create her in a way such that her body was in conflict with her soul? The suggestion is ludicrous if not blasphemous. Then did she rebel against God's plan? If so, she needs pastoral help, not encouragement in her rebellion. And the same is true for other confused young people who might hear about this case, and conclude (mistakenly, no doubt, but understandably) that the pope would support their decision to change their sexual identity.

"I wish to be clear," the pope said. "Please don't say, 'The pope sanctifies transgenders'"—a line that was omitted, curiously enough, from the Vatican summary. Unfortunately, *wishing* to be clear does not guarantee clarity. Surely the Holy Father did not set up transgender people as models. And we can all agree that the pope did not endorse sex-change operations. But if a confused young person read through the pope's answer, looking for some reason *not* to change his sexual identity, he would not find it. In the momentous battle between truth and falsehood, the defenders of truth had just been hit by friendly fire.

Many (including me) who were intrigued by Francis's fresh new approach in the first two weeks of his pontificate were worried after the first two years and by the fourth anniversary of his ascent to the throne of St. Peter were thoroughly dismayed. Meanwhile another change had taken place, largely ignored by the secular media. The crowds that had thronged to the papal audiences of 2013 began to thin out. The energetic discussions of Catholicism petered out, too. The "Francis effect" was wearing off.

Jean-Marie Guénois, the religion editor of the French daily *Le Figaro*, was probably the first journalist to spot the trend. In November 2014, when Francis traveled to Strasbourg to address the European Parliament, Guénois—who had been a member of the Vatican press corps for more than twenty years and been abroad the papal plane for more than fifty foreign trips—noticed that two things were different. First, the streets of Strasbourg were nearly empty as the papal motorcade traveled from the airport to the European Parliament. There were scarcely any people on the sidewalks to greet—or for that matter even to heckle—the pope. Second, the pope's quick trip included no events, however brief, that were open to the public. Francis addressed the Parliament, spoke to the leaders of the European Council, and quickly hopped on a flight back to Rome. Guénois concluded sadly, "The Pope did not want to see the people of Alsace, and the people of Alsace did not want to see the Pope."

On other, later papal trips, the crowds were back. During his visit to the United States the following year, for instance, the pope spoke to impressive crowds in Washington and New York, and an audience estimated at several hundred thousand greeted him in Philadelphia. The tepid public reaction to that papal visit to Strasbourg may have been an isolated incident. Still, the quick trip to Strasbourg was an indication that initial public enthusiasm for the new pope was beginning to erode.

CHAPTER THREE

Stalled Reforms

T he College of Cardinals elected Pope Francis with a mandate to reform the administration of the Holy See. They wanted an end to the "Vatileaks" that had troubled the previous pontificate and tighter control over Vatican administrators. They also wanted the new pope to advance the reforms that Pope Benedict—not a strong administrator, as he himself would acknowledge—had begun in two crucial areas: the Vatican's financial affairs and the handling of sexual-abuse complaints.

Benedict XVI had commissioned three senior cardinals to investigate the Vatileaks scandal, and their report on the problems within the Roman Curia was the subject of intense speculation before the papal conclave. Did it confirm the influence of a "gay lobby" within the Vatican? Or the existence of a cabal that was obstructing Benedict's reforms? Or financial misconduct that powerful prelates were eager to keep secret? Was the report discouraging enough to convince the aging pope that he did not have the stamina to attack the problems? All those theories were raised and discussed in the wake of Benedict's resignation. Oddly, the subject was dropped entirely from public discussions after Francis was elected.

It was Benedict who began the difficult but necessary financial reforms, installing a new management team at the troubled Vatican bank, formally known as the Institute for Religious Works, and establishing the Financial Information Authority to supervise all Vatican transactions. Against intense resistance from the Vatican bureaucracy, he allowed the Council of Europe's anti-money-laundering agency to scrutinize the Holy See's financial dealings—a decision that John Allen, the leading American Vatican-watcher, praised as "[p]erhaps the single most important" financial reform of his pontificate.

It was on the issue of sexual abuse, however, that Benedict made the most determined strides. Dissatisfied with the disciplinary actions taken (or in many cases, not taken) by various Vatican offices, he had succeeded during the last years of the reign of John Paul II in getting the responsibility for dealing with priests accused of sexual abuse moved to his own office, the Congregation for the Doctrine of the Faith. In a memorable statement before the conclave that elected him pope, Cardinal Ratzinger lamented how the face of the Church had been disfigured by the "filth" of clerical misconduct.

After his election, Benedict escalated his campaign against abusive clerics. He instructed his subordinates that he should never be photographed alongside the influential founder of the Legion of Christ, Father Marcial Maciel Degollado, who had been accused of molesting his seminarians, and ordered a high-level investigation into the complaints that had been brushed aside for years by the Mexican priest's powerful friends in the Roman Curia. As the damaging evidence mounted, Maciel was removed as head of the Legion, and in 2006 he was sentenced to spend the remainder of his life in "prayer and penance." Benedict then ordered an investigation of the religious order that Maciel had founded, to determine how much its integrity had been corrupted by the founder's double life.

The Maciel case was only one of hundreds that were adjudicated by the Vatican during the pontificate of Benedict XVI. It is true that complaints of clerical misconduct continued to pour into the Vatican as the scandal that had erupted in the United States in 2002 now hit Europe. But the vast majority of those complaints involved incidents that had taken place long ago. And as the cases percolated through the Vatican's system of justice, Benedict was unflagging in his determination to purge the "filth" from the priesthood. In 2011 and 2012 alone, he laicized (in journalistic parlance, "defrocked") nearly four hundred priests.

Reforms Derailed

The need for reform at the Vatican—for a more responsive bureaucracy, for financial transparency, and for effective discipline of clerical misconduct—did not pit liberals against conservatives. Benedict, apparently concluding that he no longer had the strength to lead a major reform, stepped down to clear the way for someone more energetic. Francis assumed the papacy with this problem foremost in his mind, and to this day he is generally regarded as a reformer.

Unfortunately, more than four years into his pontificate, Francis has failed to advance the cause of reform. On the contrary, after a promising start, he has derailed reforms that were begun under Benedict and even reforms that he initiated himself. His disdain for organization and his penchant for quick decisions have provoked several reversals of policy and heightened confusion within the Roman Curia.

Most importantly, Francis has aborted the two most critical reforms. He established the Secretariat for the Economy, giving it broad powers, and then rescinded those powers, leaving it unable to bring the desired transparency to the Vatican's finances. He set up a special panel to advise the universal Church on the handling of sexual abuse, but that panel's recommendations have not been implemented, and frustrated members have resigned—disclosing as they did so that for three years after he established the panel, the pope never met with its members. Francis himself has overlooked the failure of some of his own favorite bishops to confront abusive clerics. His dramatic reform initiatives now appear to be empty gestures, and the unhealthy clerical attitudes that Francis himself has decried so energetically have been reinforced.

The "Diseases" of the Roman Curia

Consider first the reform of the Roman Curia: the "big-ticket item" in the new pope's mandate. For more than a year after his election, Francis burnished his reputation as a crusading reformer, most notably with a stunning philippic against the failings of Vatican bureaucrats.

The pope's annual address to the Roman Curia, delivered sometime before Christmas, is usually understood as an exchange of holiday greetings and an occasion for the pontiff to share his top priorities with his closest associates. In 2005, for example, Benedict XVI used the occasion to give his famous talk against "the hermeneutic of discontinuity and rupture" in the interpretation of Vatican II, a message that became a major theme of his pontificate.

In December 2014, Francis delivered a searing critique of the "sicknesses" within the Curia, jolting Vatican-watchers (not to mention the Curia) and eliminating any possible confusion about his pastoral priorities. Reform of the Roman Curia would be his number one goal—for 2015 and probably for his entire pontificate.

The previous year's address had included a comparatively mild warning against gossip and intrigue. This time he returned to that topic but left subtlety aside as he tore into the familiar vices of bureaucracies: an inward-looking and self-important approach, careerism, pettifoggery, factionalism, and lack of a sense of humor. He spoke about the "existential schizophrenia" of Vatican officials who may be leading "a hidden, often dissolute life." And he made it abundantly clear that he was not speaking in purely abstract terms—that he believed all these failings could be found within the corridors of the Vatican.

At the end of his address the pope gave a nod to the faithful servants of the Church, mentioning that clerics, like airplanes, "only make the news when they crash." But that quick word of praise came too late to soften the overall message. Photos of the meeting show a room full of long-faced prelates. Reports indicate that the pope received only sparse, tepid applause. The mood of the pre-Christmas meeting was anything but joyous.

"I have to say, I didn't feel great walking out of that room today," one Vatican official told John Allen, who remarked that the pope's confrontational approach might be a risky one. He may want to change the way the Vatican works, but he cannot afford to alienate his entire staff or destroy morale. He needs someone to help him carry out his plans—even his plans for reform of the Roman Curia.

Francis's willingness to risk the anger of his staff, returning to the topic of the previous year's gentle rebuke and escalating his rhetoric so dramatically, suggested that the iron had entered his soul: that he had encountered resistance and was determined to overcome it.

New Offices with Unclear Powers

Just a few days before that stunning Christmas address, Jean-Marie Guénois had presciently reported in *Le Figaro* (in an article headlined "Secret War at the Vatican: How Pope Francis Is Shaking Up the Church") on a struggle between a pope determined to change the way the Vatican does business and entrenched officials equally determined to resist the changes. In a sense the Holy Father was addressing not only the Vatican staff but the Church at large, explaining to everyone why it was so important to reform the Roman Curia.

To assist him in that crusade, Francis created a new Council of Cardinals, composed of nine prelates from around the world, to study the existing structures of the Vatican and examine proposals for reform. At this writing, more than four years into the pontificate, the Council of Cardinals has met nineteen times, usually sitting in three-day sessions, poring over countless reports and recommendations, yet the actual changes in the Vatican's organizational chart have been minimal.

Francis has established two new bodies—the Dicastery for Laity, Family, and Life and the Dicastery for Promoting Integral Human Development—but neither was originally proposed by the Council of Cardinals. They developed instead from the suggestions of several cardinals in the general congregations before the conclave of 2013 and were formed by merging the duties and staffs of existing pontifical councils and commissions. Notice that both offices are designated as "dicasteries"—the blanket term for any office of the Holy See. They have no clear position in the Vatican's organizational chart, their responsibilities have not been fixed, and their staffs have not been fully integrated.

In the business world, multinational corporations can merge, shed divisions, and restructure their operations overnight. At the Vatican, four years of crusading zeal have produced only a few tentative changes, with no fundamental shift in the way business is conducted. There has been no suggestion of change in the overall structure of the Roman Curia, in which the Secretariat of State is preeminent.

Contrary to what American Catholics might assume, the Vatican Secretariat of State is not the equivalent of the U.S. State Department. It is a super-department, wielding considerable influence over all the other Vatican dicasteries except the Congregation for the Doctrine of the Faith. The Secretariat of State has two main divisions: one dealing with diplomacy, the other with internal Church affairs. The latter handles the day-to-day paperwork of the Curia. So the routine administration of the Vatican is conducted by the same office that handles relations with foreign governments.

The secretary of state is the most powerful man at the Vatican after the pope, outranking the prefects of congregations and presidents of pontifical councils. He sets the agenda for Vatican diplomacy while simultaneously controlling the flow of internal paperwork and managing the Vatican's public-relations machinery. All the important business of the Vatican flows through his office. This odd organizational structure has two important drawbacks.

First, the concentration of power in one office discourages teamwork and creativity among the other leaders of the Roman Curia and restricts the flow of information to the supreme pontiff. The pope, not his secretary of state, should make crucial policy decisions. And like any other policy maker, he could benefit from broad consultation with officials who have direct knowledge of their own fields. In the 2013 general congregations, several cardinals suggested a new office, the Moderator of the Curia—a papal chief of staff coordinating the direction of all other agencies. That proposal appears never to have gained traction with the Council of Cardinals.

Second, the combination of diplomacy and internal affairs produces an unhealthy atmosphere for the administration of the Holy See. Because clerics trained in the arts of diplomacy are the ones most likely to be influenced by worldly concerns, they should be separated from the internal administration of the Church. Vatican diplomats should understand that their job is to represent the Church to the world, not vice versa.

The Communications Revolution

The consolidation of the Vatican's media operations represents another effort at reform. In 2014 the pope formed an expert commission to study the communications needs of the Holy See and offer suggestions. According to the Vatican press office, when the Council of Cardinals reviewed the first commission's report, it "proposed to His Holiness the institution of a commission to study this final report and to suggest feasible approaches to its implementation." That announcement raised more questions than it answered. Did the first commission not offer plans for implementing its recommendations? If the ultimate goal of a reform of the Vatican's media operations is to encourage candor and clarity, it's obvious that the reforms haven't taken effect yet.

Yet there was a more important reason for concern about the announcement of the second panel. The original commission was composed of recognized experts from around the world in the fields of media and communications. The new commission was made up of clerics working in the Vatican's media operations and one executive of the newspaper owned by the Italian bishops' conference. In other words, after the Vatican had recognized the need for a thorough overhaul of its outdated, uncoordinated, and ineffective media operations, the task of implementing those proposals was assigned to a group of insiders from those same outdated, uncoordinated, and ineffective operations.

Nevertheless, efforts at reform continued, eventually producing the new Secretariat for Communications. But that new secretariat faced enormous challenges. Msgr. Dario Vigano, appointed to head the secretariat, reported in 2015 that it would take at least three years to bring all the scattered offices together into a single coordinated unit. In an unusually candid address to the staff of the secretariat in May 2017, Francis admitted that the consolidation of the many offices involved in the project would require "a little violence." It will be "good violence," the pope hastened to assure his audience, insofar as it responds to the needs of the Church in a new era of public communications.

Bringing the Vatican's communications strategy into the age of the Internet and social media was simple in comparison with the challenge of getting Vatican officials to appreciate the field of public relations. The Vatican offices involved in public communications included the newspaper *L'Osservatore Romano*, the Vatican television center, the press office, Vatican Radio, the Pontifical Council for Social Communications, and a half-dozen other offices—all operating independently, without any central strategy. Each had its own staff, its own proud history, its own interests to protect. Chris Patten, the British politician who chaired the first expert commission studying the problem, did not have to be a prophet to predict that there would be entrenched opposition to the proposed reforms.

Apart from the inevitable turf battles, the reform effort confronted knotty questions of budget and personnel. In both of those categories, the dominant concern was Vatican Radio, an enormously expensive operation with a staff of three hundred. Its employees are generally good at what they do, but what they do—what they have done, anyway—is produce radio programs. In the Vatican's new strategy for the digital age, radio broadcasts were to play a much reduced role.

But even if all the resistance could be overcome and all the turf battles settled, even if the Vatican Radio staff could adapt happily to new responsibilities and the money could be found to pay them all, the process of reform would be only beginning. The real obstacles to effective communications at the Vatican do not, and will not, lie within the reorganized Secretariat for Communications. The effort is hampered by the policies and habits of other Vatican offices on which the secretariat must rely.

Charles Collins pinpointed one of the most revealing difficulties in his analysis for the Catholic news service *Crux*:

> Sometimes a papal speech can be translated independently, in whole or in part, 3 or 4 times by different offices. Yet a central translation office hasn't been established, and it would require coordination between the new communications office, the powerful Secretariat of State, and the Pontifical Household, which controls the pope's schedule.

Control of the papal schedule was another vexed question. Before he retired from his position as director of the Vatican press office, Father Federico Lombardi admitted that he often did not know where the pope was or what he was doing. If the pope's chief spokesman doesn't know what the pontiff is doing, how can he be expected to answer the media's questions?

But often it's when the pope himself speaks that the communications problems really begin. Collins explains that "whenever the Pope speaks off the cuff—or says something controversial—the Secretariat of State tells everyone in the Vatican to wait, until the 'official version' comes out, no matter that the 'unofficial,' but authentic, version is all over television and the newswires." This problem is compounded, of course, when the pope sets aside a prepared text and speaks extemporaneously, as Francis frequently does. Reporters hear his words immediately, but hours might pass before the press office has the "official" version, vetted by the Secretariat of State—and that version might not match the statement that by now has been broadcast all over the world.

And why is the Secretariat of State involved in this process at all? Again, the secretary of state outranks everyone at the Vatican except the pope himself. Certainly Cardinal Parolin outranks Msgr. Vigano (who is, Collins notes, "the highest-ranking Vatican official to not be a bishop"). The Secretariat of State supervises every other office of the Roman Curia, and that includes the Secretariat for Communications. At any moment, then, the strategies devised by the media experts at the Secretariat for Communications can be thwarted by officials at the Secretariat of State, who are definitely not media experts.

The Vatileaks Scandal—Repeated

During the pontificate of Benedict XVI, one of the toughest public relations problems facing the Vatican was the leakage of confidential documents, and the problem has continued under Francis, exposing infighting and inefficiency—if not outright dishonesty—within the offices of the Holy See. The first Vatileaks trial, under Benedict, resulted in the conviction of his valet and left lingering suspicions of a broader conspiracy. The second scandal, dubbed "Vatileaks II," confirmed the impression that the Vatican staff was troubled by backbiting rivalries, insider deals, and flagrant misuse of the funds confided to the use of the Holy See.

The Vatileaks II scandal broke in 2015 when the Italian journalists Emiliano Fittipaldi and Gianluigi Nuzzi published books based on confidential documents obtained from sources inside the Vatican that exposed clear abuses of trust. For instance, the Congregation for the

Causes of Saints—the office that investigates candidates for beatifica-
tion and canonization—had no effective controls on spending. The
Administration of the Patrimony of the Apostolic See (APSA), the
office that administers the Vatican's extensive real estate holdings,
regularly engaged contractors without soliciting competitive bids and
offered special rates to favored tenants. Few of these complaints were
surprising to anyone who had covered the Vatican. But the specific
evidence proffered by the two journalists, drawn from confidential
documents, was evidence of another problem.

The leaks were traced, strangely enough, to a committee formed
by Francis to study the Vatican's financial affairs. In November 2015 a
Vatican prosecutor brought criminal charges against three Vatican
staffers—Msgr. Lucio Ángel Vallejo Balda, Francesca Immacolata
Chaouqui, and Nicola Maio—for leaking the internal documents. The
journalists Fittipaldi and Nuzzi were also charged with "soliciting and
exercising pressure" on the Vatican staff to furnish the documents.

The trial, before a Vatican tribunal, provided even more tabloid
fodder than the stolen documents did. Msgr. Vallejo Balda testified
that Chaouqui had seduced him and then threatened to tell all if he
did not release the documents. The flamboyant Chaouqui—whose
presence on the financial panel was difficult to explain, since she was
a publicist rather than an expert in finance—generated headlines by
alternately protesting her innocence and claiming to have more damaging secrets about the Vatican's finances. It emerged during the trial
that her husband, Corrado Lanino, controlled the computer on which
the stolen documents had been stored. In yet another strange twist,
that computer was kept in the barracks of the Swiss Guard rather than
in the office of the financial commission, apparently because of fears
that the latter was not physically secure.

In July 2016, the Vatican tribunal announced its verdicts.

Msgr. Vallejo Balda, the former secretary of the Prefecture for the
Economic Affairs of the Holy See, was convicted of leaking confidential documents to reporters. The court sentenced him to eighteen

months in prison. (In December he would be granted a papal pardon and released.)

Francesca Chaouqui, who had been described by prosecutors as the instigator of the leaks, was found guilty of conspiracy. But because the court found no conclusive evidence that she had actually given documents to reporters, she received only a ten-month sentence—to be suspended for five years. Thus Chaouqui, who had recently given birth to a son, avoided prison time.

Nicola Maio, who had been an assistant to Msgr. Vallejo Balda, was found innocent of involvement in the conspiracy.

Nuzzi and Fittipaldi, the journalists who published books based on the leaked documents, were acquitted on the grounds that since they were Italian citizens acting outside the Vatican, the court did not have jurisdiction over them.

Early in 2017, Chaouqui released her own book on the Vatileaks II affair. To no one's surprise, her account was self-serving and offered little new information, merely rehashing old stories about financial mismanagement. What was puzzling, however, was her evident determination to make the Australian Cardinal George Pell the villain of the story. Now the prefect of the Secretariat for the Economy, about which more will be said below, Cardinal Pell had become the Vatican's financial accountability czar only after the excesses that Chaouqui had recounted, and his role was to curtail the financial misadventures. So why would Chaouqui point her finger at him?

The Resistance of the Old Guard

In Morris West's novel *Shoes of the Fisherman*, an old Vatican hand gives this advice to a newly elected pope from a country far away from Rome: "Don't try to change the Romans, Holiness. Don't try to fight or convert them. They've been managing Popes for the last nineteen hundred years and they'll break your neck before you bend theirs."

Financial misconduct was only one aspect of the trouble within the Roman Curia. In their discussions leading up to the conclave of 2013, the cardinals voiced their dissatisfaction with the general culture within the Vatican bureaucracy: a dysfunctional combination of secrecy, careerism, intramural rivalries, and office politicking. Two years later, fresh leaks of confidential documents had shown that that culture persisted.

It made sense to address the Vatican's chaotic financial system first, because money is always the lifeblood of any corrupt system. The new Secretariat for the Economy, led by the imposing Cardinal Pell, was designed to make all Vatican officials accountable for their spending. But not everyone was happy with the financial reforms; Cardinal Pell ruffled feathers. So it was no surprise that when the Vatileaks II scandal broke, Andrea Tornielli, one of the best-informed Vatican journalists, had identified Pell as the target of the latest gossip.

Again, the juiciest tidbits in the new "scandal" involve incidents that occurred before Pell's appointment—incidents that were, in fact, among the main reasons for his appointment. Yes, one new book reported heavy spending in the Secretariat for the Economy. But this was an entirely new office, with broad responsibilities, needing office equipment and a full staff, including some employees with expertise in accounting and financial affairs; it was never going to be an inexpensive proposition. Perhaps more to the point, the people primarily responsible for the leaks—Vallejo Balda and Chaouqui—had evidently expected to play major roles in the new financial structures, and the leaks began after their hopes for advancement were disappointed.

Some reports have suggested that Vatileaks II demonstrated the resistance of the "old guard" to the reforming spirit of Francis. That is at best an oversimplification. The two persons who were found guilty of the leaks had been appointed by Francis himself to a commission that was intended to propose financial reforms. Vallejo Balda and Chaouqui could not simply be characterized as enemies of Francis or of economic reforms. Furthermore, there is at least some evidence that the same persons may have been involved in Vatileaks I, long before Francis arrived on the scene.

An interesting insight into Vatileaks II comes from the Vatican journalist Andrea Gagliarducci, who believes that the scandal involved a different sort of power struggle within the Curia. For years, powerful men inside the Vatican exchanged small favors with their Italian secular counterparts, Gagliarducci explains. Some of those favors involved financial transactions—the use of the Vatican bank for personal accounts, perhaps, or real estate transfers on friendly terms. Most of these little deals were harmless, but some were technically illegal, and some may have involved shady characters.

For Italian financiers, unsupervised transactions through the Vatican became more attractive after 9/11, when European banking authorities began imposing strict new regulations on Italy's banks to counteract money laundering and the financing of terrorism. Some Vatican officials—Gagliarducci refers to them as the "men of compromise"—remained willing to help out their friends, and their influence grew as the health of John Paul II deteriorated. Things came to a head when Italian banking officials began to cut ties with Vatican institutions, citing the risk of unaccountable transactions. Pope Benedict XVI responded by beginning a process of financial reform. Gagliarducci writes: "To cut a long story short, under Benedict XVI, the 'men of compromise' who played games across the Vatican-Italian financial border, lost influence."

The financial reforms that began under Benedict XVI accelerated under Francis. The prefect of the Secretariat for the Economy, Cardinal Pell, steadily increased the pressure to make all Vatican financial dealings transparent. These changes were not welcomed by the "men of compromise," who sought to undermine the reforms in general and Pell in particular.

Seen in this light, the leaks could be recognized as an attempt to embarrass the Holy See, to put public pressure on the new secretariat, and to make the reforms look wrongheaded. It was significant, then, that the latest leaks revealed questionable dealings before the reforms took effect. The goal of the leakers was not to expose wrongdoing and thereby clear the way for reform; the problems had already been identified and the solutions were being implemented. The goal, instead, was to create an impression of chaos. "In the end," Gagliarducci wrote, "the leaks seem to be the latest attempt to cast shadows on the Vatican in order to thwart Vatican reforms and exert influence over Vatican projects."

Uncontrolled Spending, Uncoordinated Budgets

To appreciate the importance of the economic reforms, one must understand that until the Secretariat for the Economy began imposing new rules, Vatican dicasteries followed no standard accounting procedures. Each office made its own spending decisions with little or no oversight. So the new Secretariat for the Economy was not merely tweaking the existing rules; it was imposing rules where none previously existed.

Francis signaled his intent to bring reform to the management of the Roman Curia when he put Cardinal Pell in charge of the secretariat. The former archbishop of Sydney was, in his youth, a star in Australian rules football, and he has never lost his combative spirit. Of all the members of the College of Cardinals, he may be the one least likely to worry about stepping on toes or about stating his blunt disagreement with any other prelate—including the pope himself.

In theory, every official of the Roman Curia serves at the pleasure of the Holy Father and has no authority except as a representative of the pope's will. In practice, however, generations of Vatican officials have been able to build up their own fiefdoms within the bureaucracy. Americans, accustomed to the notion that any official should be held accountable for his actions and decisions, often find it difficult to fathom that the Vatican operates on a much older, more personalized European system. Just as kings allowed noblemen wide latitude for conducting affairs within their own estates, pontiffs gave curial cardinals discretion over their offices. It was considered unseemly to ask a nobleman, or a cardinal of the holy Church, to justify his decisions—much less to account for his spending.

In the past this system of Vatican governance bred gross corruption: nepotism, influence-peddling, and simony. In the modern era such blatant scandals have been rare. But the potential for corruption of a subtler sort is enormous. Vatican officials routinely do favors for friends. There are lavish dinners, no-bid contracts, and expensive trips abroad. In extreme cases, this approach can give rise to the appearance, at least, of serious improprieties.

In other cases, the potential for corruption takes the form of patronage. Money—spending power—animates any bureaucracy. Officials can use discretionary spending to pursue their own ends as well as those of the institution. A powerful curial cardinal can cultivate a base of support among the bishops and religious orders that he favors.

The power to spend money is not the only source of temptation. The opportunity to receive favors or funds—gifts from wealthy individuals or institutions—can also sway a prelate's judgment. It might be too much to suggest that Vatican cardinals are venal enough to accept bribes, but some free-will gifts are unquestionably more innocent than others. Father Maciel survived for years at the helm of the Legion of Christ as investigations into his misconduct were stymied by prelates who had benefitted from his legendary fundraising.

Transparency is the enemy of corruption, real or imagined. So by imposing standard accounting procedures on every Vatican office, the Secretariat for the Economy was hoping to bring the Roman Curia into an era of accountability.

By 2015, as Cardinal Pell began his campaign for transparency, the Vatican bank was only beginning to emerge from months of turmoil prompted by complaints that the institution was providing opportunities for money laundering. The bank's obvious vulnerability—due to a lack of clear financial standards—was enough to worry Italian regulators.

"Monsignor €500"

In 2014 a financial scandal opened on another front when Msgr. Nunzio Scarano, the former director of accounting for APSA who had been suspended during a money laundering investigation, was arrested on additional money laundering charges involving an alleged plot to bring twenty million euros in cash into Italy illegally. As the case developed, prosecutors said that Scarano had offered financial services for wealthy friends: "totally private, illegal activity which was also aimed at serving outsiders." He had also reportedly solicited funds for charity from unsuspecting donors and used those funds to purchase his own luxury condominium.

Police had already taken an interest in what they described as Scarano's "enormous" financial assets. He had provoked suspicions by withdrawing €560,000 (more than $600,000) from his personal account at the Vatican bank and for asking friends to accept cash and repay him with funds that he could deposit in an Italian bank. Those transactions had triggered the initial investigation into possible violation of Italian money laundering regulations.

Scarano responded that his activities—including his special favors for wealthy clients—had all been approved by his Vatican superiors. "I never laundered dirty money, I never stole," the accused cleric insisted in a letter to the Holy Father. "I tried to help someone who asked for help." Scarano asserted that he had enough documentation to prove his innocence.

More dramatically, the monsignor charged that while working as an accountant in APSA, he had sought to curb financial misconduct by his own lay superiors in that office. His efforts were thwarted, he said, because certain cardinals were "blackmailed" and covered up the abuses.

Scarano said that he had brought the financial misconduct to the attention of Cardinal Stanisław Dziwisz, the archbishop of Krakow and former secretary to Pope John Paul II. He also said that he had contacted Cardinal Angelo Sodano, the dean of the College of Cardinals and former secretary of state. Neither prelate helped him, he said.

These claims, while obviously self-serving, were not completely implausible. How could APSA officials have failed to notice Scarano's outside activities or his lavish spending? Among friends he was known as "Monsignor €500" because of his habit of carrying wads of large-denomination bills. How could he have acquired that nickname without arousing suspicion among his colleagues at the Vatican? Before he was suspended, Scarano held a key office supervising Vatican financial accounts. If the head accountant in any corporation began showing signs of fabulous wealth, wouldn't other executives start asking questions? A *Forbes* magazine report on his case made the obvious point: "Sure, it's possible he was a rogue cleric. But Monsignor Scarano worked for two decades as a senior accountant at the Vatican, which has weathered some recent storms." It is probably not true that his superiors approved of his extracurricular activities. But it does seem clear that either his superiors were terribly negligent or that he enjoyed some sort of protection.

The Audit Suspended

The opposition to Cardinal Pell's program for financial reforms became evident in February 2015 when the world's cardinals met in a consistory to discuss the plans. "Heated arguments" reportedly erupted after the Australian outlined his proposal for the work of the new office, and several influential cardinals immediately suggested measures to scale back the authority of the secretariat. The opposition turned nasty when the first Vatileaks II documents became public, obviously designed to embarrass Pell and damage his standing. But those leaks also put Francis in an awkward position. If he wavered now in his support for Pell, he might give the leakers reason to believe that his entire program of reform could be derailed.

By approving the statutes of the new office in March of that year with only a few minor modifications, the pope signaled his support for Pell. But even as the plans moved forward, some Vatican officials, speaking anonymously, were at pains to remind reporters that the pope had not given Pell everything that he wanted. The secretariat would not oversee the Vatican's real estate holdings, for example, and there would be three auditors rather than one. But these were minor details in the context of the authority given to the secretariat. On balance the pope's decision was a clear victory for Pell.

But that victory was called into question a year later when the Vatican suddenly announced that a thorough audit by Pricewater-houseCoopers—the first outside audit of Vatican finances in history—had been suspended. Significantly, the announcement came not from the Secretariat for the Economy but from the Secretariat of State. The audit had begun in December 2015 after a preliminary inquiry uncovered the serious undervaluation of assets, unsupervised spending, and an atmosphere of mismanagement and corruption. Pressing energetically for regular audits and uniform financial controls, Pell faced resistance from other offices of the Roman Curia, and with the suspension of the PricewaterhouseCoopers audit he appeared to suffer a serious setback.

There was at first no explanation for the decision to suspend the audit. For that matter there was not any official announcement of the decision, which came to light only when the *National Catholic Register* reported on a memorandum issued on June 10, 2016, to offices of the Roman Curia by the Secretariat of State. Even Pell, who was (at least theoretically) the Vatican's top financial official, told the *Register* that he was "a bit surprised" by the decision. He expected the audit to "resume shortly," he said, but he could not make that prediction with any degree of confidence, since he did not yet know why it had been suspended.

After the audit was blocked, the Secretariat of State offered a murky explanation, suggesting that certain clauses in the auditors' contracts required further clarification and hinting that once these details were resolved, the audit could proceed. But the audit never did proceed.

By 2016 the Vatican bank was under entirely new management and well on its way to compliance with European banking regulations. Dozens of questionable accounts had been closed, new controls had been instituted, and its staff of lay professionals appeared fully committed to transparency. Unfortunately the offices of the Roman Curia were not ready to make the same commitment. Francis, who had supported the Secretariat for the Economy at first, now backed away. Visiting the offices of the new secretariat, he advised the staff to be discreet: "full accountability, yes; but let's keep our problems in-house."

The Secretariat of State now announced that an internal audit would move forward, while the services of PricewaterhouseCoopers "will also be available to those dicasteries that wish to avail themselves of its support and consulting services." In other words, those being audited would determine how far the external auditors should delve into their records.

The Secretariat of State seems to have suspended the external audit out of fear of compromising the sovereignty of the Vatican city-state—the same fear that shaped its response to the sex-abuse scandal. For the past several years a capable American lawyer, Jeffrey Lena, had been fighting off lawsuits against the Holy See by sexual-abuse victims by invoking "sovereign immunity." A sovereign state does not have to respond to private plaintiffs in a court of law. And a sovereign state—as the June 10 announcement reminded us—does not open its books to an external auditor.

But there was a price to be paid for sovereign immunity. Did the Holy See wish to be seen by the world primarily as a sovereign state or as a spiritual stronghold? While Francis spoke frequently about a

"Church that is poor," about reforming the Curia and dismantling its fiefdoms, and about his willingness to "make a mess," would the institutional prerogatives of the Vatican bureaucracy take precedence over the Church's evangelizing mission?

A Turf Battle between Financial Agencies

By a *motu proprio* (an executive order of the pope "on his own initiative") later that year, the pope returned the responsibility for the Vatican's financial assets to the Administration of the Patrimony of the Apostolic See. The Secretariat for the Economy would exercise oversight: establishing procedures for financial transactions and ensuring that those procedures were followed. Francis explained that he wanted to separate administration from financial oversight. "It is of the utmost importance that bodies responsible for vigilance are separated from those that are being overseen," he wrote. But the *motu proprio* put financial management back in the hands of the agency whose top accountant had been "Monsignor €500." It was a major victory for the officials who argued that Cardinal Pell was asserting too much control in his bid to ensure financial accountability.

The turf battle between the Secretariat for the Economy and APSA would continue. APSA evidently decided to proceed with an audit on its own terms, effectively denying the supervisory role of the Secretariat for the Economy. Msgr. Mauro Rivella, the secretary of APSA, instructed dicasteries to provide data to PricewaterhouseCoopers, saying that the accounting firm was conducting an audit of Vatican finances. In May 2017, Pell complained that APSA had overstepped its authority, and he quickly wrote to all the same offices, telling them that APSA had "no authority, nor prerogative," to issue such instructions. The cardinal's letter—also signed by Libero Milone, the Vatican's auditor general—told Vatican officials "with deep regret" that they should not comply with the APSA directive. Pell pointed out that the external audit by PricewaterhouseCoopers had been suspended more than a year earlier, and "there is no ongoing audit" by outside accountants.

The tensions between APSA and the Secretariat for the Economy had been aggravated, Edward Pentin of the *National Catholic Register* reported, because APSA had not complied with requests for information from the secretariat. Pell remarked that the conflict had provoked a "moment of truth" for the cause of Vatican economic reform. The campaign for transparency had lost momentum, and in an atmosphere still marked by intramural battles and unassailable private fiefdoms, it seemed only a matter of time before some new financial scandal would emerge.

In yet another setback for the cause of financial reform, the Vatican's auditor general, Libero Milone, resigned in June, just a few weeks after the struggle between APSA and the Secretariat for the Economy became public. The terse announcement of his departure, with no explanation offered, and the notice that a search for Milone's replacement would begin "as soon as possible" suggested that his resignation was not planned in advance. Italian media reported that he had recently been offered a post as director of the Italian broadcasting network but had turned it down, saying that he wanted to focus on his responsibilities at the Vatican.

Several weeks after Milone's departure, in September 2017, he disclosed to reporters that he had been forced to resign after he probed into evidence of financial misconduct by an important Vatican official, whom Milone, bound by a confidentiality agreement, declined to identify. The assistant secretary of state, Archbishop Giovanni Becciu, called this charge "false and unjustified," yet the archbishop confirmed that he had given Milone a choice between resigning quietly and facing criminal charges for "spying on the private lives of his superior and staff."

If Milone was "spying" on other Vatican officials, he may have had good reason to do so. Suspecting that his office had been bugged and its computers hacked, he brought in an outside contractor to investigate. When the contractor confirmed that a computer in the auditor's office had been compromised, Milone instructed him to broaden his investigation and identify the culprit. In other words, having learned that he was under surveillance, he indulged in a bit of counter-surveillance.

Responding to Milone's disclosures, an official Vatican statement charged that the auditor general had "illegally engaged an external company to conduct investigative activities on the private life of Holy See personnel." The key word here is "illegally." Had Milone exceeded his authority, violating the statutes that governed his role? A Reuters report offered an interesting observation:

> It was not clear which statutes were said to have been violated. Article two of the statutes says the auditor-general has "full autonomy and independence," including to "receive and investigate any reports on anomalous activities" of Vatican entities.

As I write, three months after Milone's departure, the office of the auditor general remains unoccupied. In theory the auditor general would work under the prefect of the Secretariat for the Economy. But Cardinal Pell's indefinite leave of absence to defend himself against sexual abuse charges in Australia leaves that office empty too. If no one at the highest levels of the Vatican feels an urgent need to fill these positions, even with temporary administrators, then the campaign for financial accountability seems to have been suspended.

Coping with the Sex-Abuse Scandal

Vatican insiders may see financial transparency as the key to more responsible stewardship within the Roman Curia, but from the outside, it appears that the most urgently needed reforms are those involving the handling of sexual abuse accusations.

The tightening of disciplinary procedures for clerics accused of sexual misconduct began with the American hierarchy in 2002 and accelerated through the pontificate of Benedict XVI. But two related problems remain unaddressed. First, the Vatican has not yet ensured that the same "zero-tolerance" policy will be in force, and that abuse complaints will be promptly addressed, in every ecclesiastical jurisdiction throughout the world. Some bishops have lagged in their responses to the crisis.

Second, and more important, the Vatican has not yet established an effective policy for dealing with bishops who neglect their responsibility to deal with predatory priests. As I explained in my book *The Faithful Departed*, the negligence of many Catholic bishops—and worse, their deliberate efforts to mislead the faithful by covering up evidence of abuse—was more damaging to the credibility of the Church than the abuse itself. The sexual abuse of young people is a crime and a terrible sin, but the Church has a long acquaintance with individuals' sins. It was Church leaders' siding with the predators at the expense of their victims and lying to protect the criminals that shook confidence in the entire institution. If bishops would lie about such things, how could they be trusted on other subjects? And if the bishops were not trustworthy, how could we know that we were receiving the true Faith, passed down from the apostles?

During Francis's pontificate, the Vatican has been confronted by accusations of sexual abuse against two prominent prelates. Neither case has yet produced a clear result—although not through any lack of diligence on the part of the Vatican.

The first case involves Józef Wesołowski, a Polish archbishop and Vatican diplomat who in 2013 was accused of molesting boys while serving as the papal nuncio to the Dominican Republic. Recalled to the Vatican, Wesołowski was laicized in the first stage of canonical proceedings. Prosecutors in the Dominican Republic and Poland had expressed interest in bringing criminal charges against him, but the Holy See chose to continue its own proceedings with a criminal trial, reasoning that the former nuncio was immediately subject to Vatican law. The criminal trial was postponed, however, when Wesołowski—who was under house arrest at the Vatican—fell ill. He died in August 2015 before the trial could resume.

The second case is that of Archbishop Anthony Apuron of Agaña, in Guam. He too was accused of molesting boys and in June 2016 was relieved of his administrative duties and summoned to Rome. As complaints against Apuron multiplied, Archbishop Savio Hon Tai Fai, named temporary caretaker of the Church in Guam, announced that he had urged the Holy See to remove Apuron permanently from his post and appoint a successor. Taking a step in that direction in October, the Vatican named Michael Byrnes, an auxiliary bishop of Detroit, coadjutor archbishop of Agaña "with special faculties," indicating that he would take over the administration of the Guam archdiocese immediately and succeed Apuron should the suspended archbishop be formally stripped of his office. Meanwhile a Vatican investigation of Apuron's conduct was underway as of this writing.

In these two cases the Vatican demonstrated a stern resolve to discipline abusive bishops. Still the question remained: would the Holy See be equally firm in taking action against bishops who had not abused young people themselves but had been negligent in curbing abuse by priests under their jurisdiction?

Holding Bishops Accountable for Sex-Abuse Complaints

The pope's own record is not impressive in this regard. In 2015 he promoted a Chilean prelate, Bishop Juan Barros, over loud protests that Barros had ignored complaints of abuse by a priest who was his friend. Angry Catholics demonstrated at the cathedral in Osorno, where Barros was to be installed, and a delegation of other Chilean bishops visited the Vatican to question the appointment. But Francis held firm, insisting that Barros was innocent of misconduct. He was caught on film saying that the Chilean Catholics were "stupid" to believe the complaints against Barros.

Later that year, the pontiff appointed his ally Cardinal Godfried Danneels to participate in the Synod of Bishops. There was no evident reason for the retired Belgian archbishop to be given such an active role. Indeed, there were compelling reasons for excluding him from a discussion of family life. Several years earlier Danneels had been the object of a Belgian police investigation into sexual abuse that culminated in a raid on archdiocesan offices and a search of the cardinal's residence. No criminal charges were filed, but police had evidently suspected that the cardinal was concealing evidence of abuse. Indeed, Belgian newspapers published transcripts of a conversation, secretly recorded, in which the cardinal had urged a man to remain silent about the abuse he had suffered at the hands of another Belgian prelate. Confronted with that evidence, the cardinal's office could only offer Danneel's limp admission that "the whole approach...was not the right one."

In 2014, Francis intervened in the case of Mauro Inzoli, an Italian priest who had been stripped of his clerical status by the Congregation for the Doctrine of the Faith (CDF) after he was found guilty of molesting adolescents. The pope, responding to pleas from a few of his close advisers, overruled that decision, though he was forced to reverse his own decision and laicize Inzoli after an Italian court found him guilty of multiple counts of sexual abuse.

So would Francis approve a policy that holds bishops accountable for their negligence? He seemed to answer that question in June 2015 with new disciplinary norms for bishops who fail to act on sexual abuse complaints. Recommended by a special papal commission headed by Cardinal Sean O'Malley of Boston, endorsed by the Council of Cardinals, and conditionally approved by the pope for five years, the norms would subject such bishops to the jurisdiction of a new tribunal under the CDF. Francis also approved the allocation of "adequate resources" to staff the new tribunal, which would also assist the CDF in cases involving sexual abuse by other clerics, for which it was already responsible.

Then a curious thing happened—nothing. No tribunal was established, no staff was assigned, no office space was set aside. No steps whatsoever were taken to carry out the policy that Francis had approved.

A year passed quietly, and then at last Francis issued a new policy. As he had done with the Secretariat for the Economy—endowing it with sweeping powers that he later trimmed back because of internal resistance—the pope rescinded his approval of the new norms. In a *motu proprio* of June 2016, the pope declared that there was no need for a new tribunal to handle disciplinary cases against negligent bishops because the Code of Canon Law already provides adequate remedies. All that was needed, therefore, was a clarification that the existing procedures for disciplining bishops "for grave causes" may be applied to bishops who fail to curtail abuse of minors by clerics. In announcing this new policy, the pope did not even mention the old one. But the tribunal announced in June 2015 was clearly a dead letter in June 2016.

The new policy raised two obvious questions. First, if canon law already allowed for disciplinary action against bishops, why had a new tribunal been erected? Second, if the disciplinary mechanism had been in place all along, why had no bishops been punished? As Father Alexander Lucie-Smith, writing in London's *Catholic Herald*, concluded, "So it can be done. What is needed is the will to do it."

If that conclusion was somewhat cynical, Cardinal O'Malley unintentionally vindicated such cynicism when he remarked that the *motu proprio* conveyed "a sense of urgency and clarity that was not there before." Really? Had it taken fifteen years of catastrophe to arouse a "sense of urgency" sufficient for a clarification of canonical guidelines? If Cardinal O'Malley intended to be reassuring, he failed miserably.

A Commission without Support

In February 2017, the Associated Press reported on the work of O'Malley's commission. The news was discouraging. In a paragraph inexplicably buried at the bottom of the article, the story revealed that the commission's work was ignored:

Francis scrapped the commission's proposed tribunal for
bishops who botch abuse cases following legal objections
from the congregation. The commission's other major initiative—a guideline template to help dioceses develop policies to fight abuse and safeguard children—is gathering
dust. The Vatican never sent the template to bishops' conferences, as the commission had sought, or even linked it to its
main abuse-resource website.

This shocking report followed close on the heels of complaints,
aired by two members of the papal commission, that the group had
been overworked and underfunded and that meetings were not held
regularly. But the AP report was far more damaging, showing that the
commission had launched two important projects, and neither had
been implemented.

It was appalling that negligent bishops still were not being held
accountable, though any recommendation for disciplining bishops was
bound to face stiff opposition. But now it came to light that the papal
commission had not even managed to post its own recommendations
on its own website.

A few weeks later Marie Collins, a member of the commission who
was herself a victim of abuse, resigned, complaining that the group's
work had been thwarted from within the Roman Curia. A few days
after her public announcement, Cardinal Gerhard Müller, the prefect
of the Congregation for the Doctrine of the Faith—which was the main
target of Collins's criticism—defended the CDF and denied any foot-
dragging on the abuse issue. Collins quickly shot back, rebutting the
cardinal's arguments.

Bear in mind that Collins's resignation was not a bolt from the blue.
She had frequently shown signs of impatience. Nor was she the first
member of the commission to leave. Peter Saunders—who, like Collins,
is an abuse victim—had been asked to resign in 2016 after issuing a
series of angry comments. Refusing, he was placed involuntarily on an

indefinite "leave of absence." Another member, Claudio Papale, resigned in September 2016 without any public explanation.

In her resignation announcement, Collins cited the scuttling of the tribunal for negligent bishops and the failure to implement worldwide guidelines as sources of frustration. But the "last straw," she said, had been the CDF's refusal to implement a recommendation from the commission that every abuse victim who contacts the Vatican receive a personal reply from Rome. Cardinal Müller's entirely reasonable response was that personal contact with abuse victims should be the responsibility of local bishops, not officials in Rome. The CDF hears hundreds of abuse cases, originating in dioceses all around the world. It seems unrealistic to expect that the CDF become familiar with every person involved. An American who appeals his case to the Supreme Court expects a fair hearing but not a personal note from one of the justices.

In his response to other complaints, however, Müller was less compelling. He characterized the tribunal for bishops as a mere proposal rather than an established fact. Yet Vatican Radio had announced in June 2015, "Pope Francis has created a new Vatican tribunal section to hear cases of bishops who fail to protect children from sexually abusive priests," and the Vatican press office had reported, "The Council of Cardinals agreed unanimously on these proposals and resolved that they be submitted to the Holy Father, Pope Francis, who approved the proposals and authorized the provision of sufficient resources for this purpose."

But of course the tribunal had not been set up, and now, months later, Müller explained the odd sequence of events. After the pope had approved the tribunal, Vatican officials discussed the plan and concluded that the disciplinary task could be handled by the Congregation for Bishops (and the Congregation for the Eastern Churches for bishops of the Eastern rites, or the Congregation for Evangelization for those in mission territories). So Collins's complaint was at least partially correct—the Roman Curia did block the implementation of the O'Malley commission's plan.

Still Müller could justifiably argue that the fundamental goal of the papal commission—the establishment of a means to discipline negligent bishops—had been achieved. Evidently Francis was convinced that the approach recommended by the Roman Curia was superior to the approach he had approved a year earlier. It was odd, however, that the Curia had apparently discussed that approach only after the initial proposal had been approved. In another display of the chaotic administrative style that has characterized this pontificate, the O'Malley commission, the Council of Cardinals, and the pope had instituted an important new policy without having consulted the officials most closely involved.

In her answer to Müller, Marie Collins produced other evidence that the O'Malley commission was not working closely with other Vatican offices. She complained that CDF officials did not attend the commission's meetings or respond to invitations for discussions. The picture that emerged was of a papal commission detached from the regular offices of the Vatican: a commission that could not persuade other Vatican officials to cooperate or even to post its recommendations on the Holy See's website.

Marie Collins charged that the Roman Curia was not in sympathy with the papal commission, and in his response, Müller indirectly lent credence to that complaint by implying that the commission did not recognize the realities of the work at the Vatican. So was the commission being unreasonable, or was the CDF being intransigent? In an important sense it did not matter. One way or another, two important Vatican bodies were not cooperating. And the failure of anyone to make them cooperate by clear directives from above suggested that—rhetoric aside—ending the sex-abuse scandal still was not a top papal priority.

In September 2017, Francis finally met with the commission that he had established in 2014. He acknowledged that the Church had been "late" in responding to the problem of sexual abuse and that the commission had been forced to "swim against the tide." The pope made the remarkable confession that he himself was "learning on the job"—learning, for example, to accept a "zero tolerance" policy fifteen years after the sexual abuse scandals had exploded. But while he encouraged the commission in its work and was pleased that some episcopal conferences had accepted the commission's recommendations, the pope offered no new promises. Marie Collins responded to the pope's remarks by saying, "Zero tolerance is the way to go, but it's toothless if there isn't a sanction for anyone who doesn't operate it."

Playing Favorites

Disturbing as it is that the campaign for reform has bogged down, it is still more disturbing that Francis has shown a pronounced tendency to exempt his own allies from such reforms as he has proposed, thereby rendering those reforms ineffectual. The Vatican has a long and unhappy history of allowing prelates to escape the consequences of their own missteps; any successful Vatican reform must begin with a determination to hold Church officials accountable. The high cost of playing favorites was illustrated by two damaging incidents that became public in the summer of 2017, just before this book went to press.

First, the Vatican indicted two former officials of the Bambino Gesù Hospital (which is owned and operated by the Holy See) on embezzlement charges. This indictment was the first such action brought by Vatican prosecutors under the new rules designed to promote transparency and accountability in financial transactions. The Vatican had been under pressure from European banking authorities to prosecute violations of these rules.

Giuseppe Profiti and Massimo Spina—the president and treasurer, respectively, of the Bambino Gesù Foundation—were charged with improperly spending more than four hundred thousand euros in foundation funds on the renovation of an apartment owned by Cardinal Tarcisio Bertone. Investigators unearthed a series of financial transactions that suggested a contractor was paid by two different Vatican offices for his work in a case that has given rise to the Vatican's first indictments for financial misconduct. The contractor, Gianantonio Bandera—who was recommended for the job by Cardinal Bertone—eventually filed for bankruptcy and did not complete the renovations. Neither Bandera nor Cardinal Bertone was named as a defendant in the case.

The indictment came just a week after an Associated Press report uncovered evidence of serious mismanagement at the Bambino Gesù Hospital in the past: mismanagement that had compromised the quality of patients' care. Vatican officials said that the report had been exaggerated and that the existing problems had been addressed by new hospital administrators.

In the second scandal, Vatican police broke up a drug-fueled homosexual orgy in the apartment of the private secretary to Cardinal Francesco Coccopalmerio, the president of the Pontifical Council for Legislative Texts. It is not clear how the secretary, Msgr. Luigi Capozzi, had landed an apartment in a residence reserved for the highest-ranking Vatican officials. Apparently he had influential friends, and there were reports that he was in line for appointment as a bishop.

Capozzi had access to a car with Vatican license plates, another sign of influential friends, which made him virtually exempt from searches by the Italian police and could have facilitated the transportation of illegal drugs. The location of his residence—in a building with one door leading onto Vatican territory, the other onto the streets of Rome—was also ideal for someone avoiding police oversight. He finally pushed too far, however. Other residents of the building (presumably including some of those top Vatican officials) complained about a steady train of young male visitors and of noisy parties at Capozzi's apartment. Those complaints prompted the police raid.

These two cases—one financial scandal, one sexual scandal—drew attention to the unfinished business of Vatican reform. Could Catholics be confident that the financial affairs of the Bambino Gesù

Hospital were now in order? Or that no more powerful Vatican figures were being protected from prosecution? Did the unsavory career of Msgr. Capozzi signal the enduring power of a "gay lobby" within the Vatican? Effective Vatican reforms might have provided satisfactory answers to these questions.

CHAPTER FOUR

Manipulating the Synod

Worries about Pope Francis's provocative statements and his commitment to upholding Church doctrine came to a head with an extraordinary assembly of the Synod of Bishops in 2014 and the ordinary assembly of the Synod in 2015. Until then he had issued few authoritative documents, but the papal document that would follow the two assemblies would be a statement that could not be dismissed: a formal expression of the Church's Magisterium.

The Synod is an advisory body of bishops from around the world—some selected by the pontiff, others chosen by their peers in the various national episcopal conferences—established (or revived) by Pope Paul VI after the Second Vatican Council. It meets in "ordinary" assemblies every three or four years to consider an important matter in the life of the Church, issuing a final statement after a few weeks of deliberation. Though not authoritative in itself, that statement becomes the basis for a "post-synodal apostolic exhortation" by the pope, a teaching document that carries a high level of teaching authority.

The assembly of the Synod follows months of preparation. A topic is chosen and the Vatican's permanent office of the Synod prepares a series of questions to be discussed. These questions are circulated among the world's bishops for comment, and their suggestions are incorporated into a second working document, which serves as the basis for the Synod discussions.

An ordinary meeting of the Synod was scheduled for October 2015, the topic being marriage and family life. Francis decided to call an "extraordinary" session to meet in October 2014, giving this crucial topic a double dose of discussion. That decision seemed eminently reasonable, in light of the extraordinary assault on family life in the early twenty-first century: the high rate of family breakdown and divorce, the rising incidence of cohabitation and promiscuity, the routine acceptance of abortion and contraception, the drive for legal recognition of same-sex unions.

As the preparations began, however, it became clear that Francis had a different priority for this Synod. He had called a consistory—a meeting of the College of Cardinals—for February 2014, at which he would appoint new members to the college. As is now customary, the cardinals assembled in Rome the day before the consistory for a general discussion. Francis had asked a German prelate, Cardinal Walter Kasper, the retired president of the Pontifical Council for Christian Unity, to address them.

The "Kasper Proposal" Tops the Agenda

This suggestion, which came to be known as the "Kasper proposal," strikes at the heart of two essential Catholic teachings. First, since the earliest days of Christianity, the Church has taught that anyone who receives the Eucharist while in a state of grave sin commits another grave sin of sacrilege. St. Paul wrote in his first letter to the Corinthians, "Whoever, therefore, eats the bread or drinks the cup of the Lord in an unworthy manner will be guilty of profaning the Body and Blood of the Lord" (11:27–28). Second, the Church has always taught that anyone who remarries while his spouse from a valid marriage is still alive is living in a state of grave sin.[1] This discipline is based not on an

---

1 A decree of nullity, commonly called an "annulment," is a finding by a Church tribunal that a putative marriage is not valid—that is, that there never was a marriage. A valid marriage can never be "dissolved."

arbitrary rule but on the clear words of Jesus himself: "But I say to you that every one who divorces his wife, except on the grounds of unchastity, makes her an adulteress, and whoever marries a divorced woman commits adultery" (Matthew 5:32).

Francis opened the February 2014 consistory—his first meeting with the full College of Cardinals since his election nearly a year earlier—by underlining the Church's teaching that the family, based on marriage, is "the fundamental cell of human society." Observing that in our era the family "is regarded with disdain and maltreated," he urged Church leaders to work to restore the "recognition of how beautiful, true, and good it is to form a family." Then he introduced Cardinal Kasper, who spoke for nearly two hours, taking up almost all of a morning session.

Father Federico Lombardi, the director of the Vatican press office, told reporters that Kasper's remarks were intended for the cardinals and would not be made public, but he did provide a brief summary of the talk. Kasper's thoughts were very much "in harmony" with those of Francis, Lombardi said, and emphasized the role of the family as a domestic church and as an instrument for evangelization. Kasper had spoken about the understanding of marriage and family in Christian theology: established at creation, damaged by sin, but raised to the level of a sacrament and redeemed by grace. Lombardi confirmed that Cardinal Kasper did broach the subject that had commanded much media attention: the status of Catholics who are divorced and remarried. Without providing details of the cardinal's thoughts, Lombardi said that Kasper had invoked Benedict XVI, who had urged greater pastoral care for Catholics in these situations, and Francis, who had said that the question of pastoral care should not be seen as in opposition to the canonical question of the validity of a marriage. Kasper closed his address, Lombardi said, by speaking of the "law of gradualness," exploring how married couples could come eventually to a deeper understanding of their sacramental bond and a better appreciation for their family life.

Andrea Tornielli provided a more detailed account of Kasper's speech. Based on reports from cardinals who were in attendance, Tornielli said that Kasper had challenged the prelates to address the problem of Catholics who are divorced and remarried. The Church cannot change her doctrine regarding the indissolubility of marriage, the cardinal said. But pastors can and should find ways to reach out to Catholics in irregular marriages. He stressed that no situation is too difficult to allow for God's mercy.

Tornielli also reported that Kasper had expressed misgivings about proposals to ease access to the Church tribunals that issue annulments, fearing that a streamlined annulment process would lead to fresh complaints that the Church was accommodating a hypocritical sort of "Catholic divorce." But he asked whether it might be possible to allow for some sort of penitential process by which Catholics who are divorced and remarried could be reconciled with the Church, just as the early Church provided a penitential process to allow the re-entry of those who had renounced their faith to escape persecution.

Another German, Cardinal Reinhard Marx, the archbishop of Munich and Freising, quickly suggested that the Kasper proposal should be made public. He noted that Francis had applauded the presentation, saying that Kasper had raised "profound" issues. Moreover, some two hundred copies of the speech were already in circulation, having been distributed to the cardinals at the consistory, so it was inevitable that its content should become public.

In early March, Kasper announced in a Vatican Radio interview that he would indeed make his thoughts public in a book to be published in German and Italian. This project had the approval of the pope, he said, who "wanted an open discussion about an urgent problem." "I maintain the full teaching of the Church," he assured his interviewer, "but the teaching has to be applied to concrete situations." The Church must find ways "to help, support, and encourage" divorced and remarried Catholics, and his own suggestion was an attempt to do so while avoiding both "rigorism" and "laxism."

What the World Needed to Hear

As it became apparent that the Kasper proposal would be a primary topic for the extraordinary Synod meeting in October, defenders of the traditional Church teaching mobilized. In the United States, Ignatius Press rushed out three books, including a volume of essays by prominent scholars and prelates directly rebutting the Kasper proposal. (The publication of this book would occasion a brief but revealing dispute at the Synod meeting, as I explain below.) Cardinal Raymond Burke, an American who then served as prefect for the Apostolic Signatura, the highest canonical court, took the lead in critiquing the Kasper proposal, telling an Irish audience that its adoption would "constitute a change in Church teaching, which is impossible." He went on to say that it was "outrageous" to suggest that criticism of the Kasper proposal was really criticism of Pope Francis.

Outrageous or not, the world's media outlets spread the word that Francis was seeking a change in Church teaching—or at the least a dramatic change in discipline—as the October meeting approached. By the time the bishops assembled in Rome, the Kasper proposal had come to dominate public discussion.

The disproportionate attention paid to this one proposal, regardless of its merits, revealed a serious imbalance in the Synod's approach. At a time when marriage and the family were under unprecedented attack—a crisis threatening our entire civilization—the bishops of the Catholic world appeared fixated on a nicety of Church law. Worse, by concentrating on this debate they squandered an opportunity to deliver the one message that our society most desperately needs to hear.

As the Synod fathers were opening their discussions in Rome, the U.S. Supreme Court announced that it would not hear appeals of lower-court decisions that had overturned state marriage laws. The result of those decisions was that the very term "marriage" had an entirely new legal meaning in thirty states, while the remaining twenty states (for the time being) held to the traditional definition. American society no longer had a common understanding of what marriage *is*.

Americans were not alone in their confusion. All around the Western world, politicians and jurists were directing the public to accept same-sex unions—which only a decade or two ago were universally recognized as disordered—as equal to male-female marriages.

Ideas have consequences, and so it should be no surprise that as we lost our theoretical understanding of what constitutes real marriage we also lost our practical ability to hold marriages together. The widespread acceptance of divorce—as a common occurrence, not just a last resort in exceptional circumstances—was the first sign of that failure. But the problem grew dramatically with the adoption of "no-fault" divorce laws, which made it possible for one party to sever a marriage contract. As the political scientist Stephen Baskerville has observed, "Today it is not possible to form a binding agreement to create a family." By making the permanent contract of marriage terminable at will, the state actually redefined marriage about fifty years ago.

Baskerville has rightly complained that "the churches have never raised their voices against the state's usurpation of power" in redefining marriage through divorce laws, and the Synod of Bishops would do nothing to change that when it met in 2014 and 2015. The problem of easy divorce never came up.

Real marriage requires real commitment. Over the past generation the West has seen a spectacular rise in the number of couples who prefer to live together without marrying: acting like spouses but declining to make a commitment. These are unstable unions, and intentionally so: either partner can leave at any time to form another relationship. At the same time, the rate of out-of-wedlock birth has skyrocketed. Today the rate of illegitimacy among *all* newborn American babies is over 40 percent.

Divorce and illegitimacy have produced an unprecedented situation in which most children, in the United States and in many European countries, are not living in households headed by their married parents. These children will face many handicaps in life, including the lack of models who might help them to build stable, lasting marriages of their own. There is no more certain recipe for a dysfunctional society than a population dominated by the children of broken homes. And that is what we now have.

Yet for some revolutionary thinkers, that is not enough. "Gender ideology"—the notion that one's sexual identity is entirely a matter of one's own choice—is rapidly gaining influence in the schools. This bizarre ideology, now worming its way into primary schools, subverts any understanding that men and women, fathers and mothers, are distinguishable—any notion that the family matters at all.

Assessing the gravity of the crisis, Msgr. Cormac Burke writes:

> While not pessimistic by nature, I must say that we are blinking at reality if we do not face up to the fact that since the 1950s, marriage and the family, outside and inside the Church, have been plunged into an ever-growing crisis—to the extent that their nature, and very existence, are threatened by total collapse.

A longtime judge of the Roman Rota, the Church's highest appellate court, Msgr. Burke has as much experience evaluating shattered marriages as anyone. "If I had to sum up the causes of this crisis in one factor," he writes, "it would be this: *marriage is no longer approached as a family enterprise*. It has become basically a 'you-and-me' affair" [His emphasis].

Real marriage has three essential characteristics: it is faithful, fruitful, and for life. Burke's analysis points us toward the second of these characteristics. If a couple enter into a union intent only on satisfying their own needs and desires, they are missing a vital ingredient: the orientation toward children. Thus we arrive at the great secret of Catholic teaching on marriage: the need to be open to life.

In the explosion of protest that greeted *Humanae Vitae*, Pope Paul VI's 1968 encyclical reaffirming the Church's traditional condemnation of artificial contraception, most Catholic leaders ran for cover, abandoning the public defense of the link between marriage and children. Speaking to the *Wall Street Journal* just a few months before the Synod convened in 2014, New York's Cardinal Timothy Dolan confessed that the Catholic hierarchy had missed a crucial opportunity by failing to take up the message of *Humanae Vitae*: "We forfeited the chance to be a coherent moral voice when it comes to one of the more burning issues of the day."

Today the burning issue is: What constitutes marriage? If that question is answered incorrectly, healthy family life becomes the exception rather than the rule. Without healthy families, our civilization is doomed.

The only institution that can lead the recovery of a proper understanding of marriage and the family is the Church. But the Synod of Bishops chose to focus on how to accommodate divorced and remarried Catholics rather than on why so many Catholics no longer understand the indissolubility of marriage or even the authority of the Ten Commandments.

As critical as it is to defend the integrity of the family, the Catholic Church goes even further in teaching that a sacramental marriage is a reflection of God's love for his people; the Church is the Bride of Christ. As the *Catechism of the Catholic Church* puts it, "The sacrament of matrimony signifies the union of Christ and his Church." Any suggestion, therefore, that the marital bond may be broken or somehow fade away implies that Christ's love for the Church might also lapse.

Transparency in Theory, Manipulation in Fact

Even before the Synod fathers arrived in Rome at the start of October 2014, everyone knew that the proceedings would revolve around one central question: Would the pope and his favorite theologian be able to overcome the resistance of the Vatican's old guard and drive through a change in the Church's practice regarding marriage and divorce? It remained to be seen whether this contest would take place on an even playing field.

In his address to the bishops on their first day of discussions, the pope seemed to indicate that it would. He urged the Synod fathers to speak out boldly, "without human respect, without timidity." The secretary general of the Synod, Cardinal Lorenzo Baldisseri, echoed that message, declaring that "discussion at the Synod is to be open." The reality, however, was dramatically different. The Synod meeting of October 2014 was far *less* transparent than previous sessions.

In the past, reporters had been allowed to attend the working sessions. The bishops' addresses were translated into several languages and made public. The talks may have been long and dry; the discussion may have been disjointed. But anyone who wanted to know what was happening at the Synod could easily find a full record of the proceedings.

For this session, though, the Vatican press office provided only a short summary of the day's proceedings. The arguments that took up several hours were compressed into a few paragraphs. A few direct quotations might be included in the summaries, but the speakers were not identified. Which prelates made which points? Observers could only guess.

These summaries ensured that the outside world heard nothing about the Synod that was not filtered through the Vatican press office. If the officials who prepared the summaries did not find an argument worthy of mention, no one ever heard about it. Rather than being instructed by the Synod fathers themselves, journalists were being instructed by the press office.

Such censorship nearly always backfires, however. There are always leaks. There are always enterprising reporters looking for inside information and sources ready to supply it. When everything is on the record, honest reporters can sort through the arguments and rebuttals, note the identity of the key participants in the debate, and reach logical conclusions about the trends of the discussion. When information is at a premium, however, insiders can advance their particular agendas by playing up their own arguments and casting their opponents in an unfavorable light.

Synod officials said the restrictions were intended to *encourage* candor. If the sessions were closed, they reasoned, bishops would not feel inhibited about speaking plainly. With no reporters in the audience, they could be blunt, confident that their disputes would not be splashed across the next day's headlines.

But what harm would there be in the world's seeing Catholic bishops in a heated debate? Why not let the differences of opinion—which everyone knew about—be a matter of public record?

Cardinal Gerhard Müller of the Congregation for the Doctrine of the Faith had argued for a more open approach. "All Christians have the right to be informed about the interventions by their bishops," he said. Those who followed the Synod debates could learn from the bishops' disagreements, gaining a deeper understanding of the issues.

Despite the official secrecy, highly colored accounts of the proceedings began to appear in the mass media. As the Synod fathers wondered which of their colleagues might have been sources, the atmosphere of trust began to deteriorate. Robert Royal, an American Catholic writer and commentator who had covered several previous Synod meetings, reported that the atmosphere in Rome was unusually tense, the comments heard in cafes often bitter, sometimes shockingly nasty.

The tension and even bitterness were aggravated, at least in the more conservative circles, by a glaring double standard in the calls for an open, unfettered discussion. Cardinal Burke, a model of speaking "without human respect, without timidity," was the object of rumors—which proved to be accurate—that the pope was about to signal his disfavor by removing him from his influential post as the head of the Apostolic Signatura and consigning him to a less important position. Meanwhile Cardinal Kasper was ubiquitous in the media, promoting his argument that the Church should allow Catholics who are divorced and remarried to receive Communion. Reliable sources revealed that Cardinal Müller, whose job was to safeguard Catholic doctrine, had been told that he must not promote a book in which he criticized the Kasper proposal.

The Mystery of the Purloined Volumes

Müller was one of the five cardinals who contributed chapters to the book *Remaining in the Truth of Christ*, in which an array of scholars argued that the Kasper proposal was incompatible with the teaching and pastoral practice of the Church. Father Robert Dodaro, an American patristics scholar in Rome, worked closely with Cardinal Burke in assembling the volume, which was published by Ignatius Press of San Francisco, led by the Jesuit priest Joseph Fessio.

Hoping to shed some light on the Synod's discussions in October, Father Fessio sought to put advance copies of the book into the hands of the participants. Many of them were staying at the Vatican's St. Martha residence, but others had found their own accommodations, and those who were full-time residents of Rome would commute to the meetings from their own apartments. The office of the Synod had local addresses for all the participants but refused to release that list.

With the addresses it was able to find on its own, Ignatius Press sent copies of the book to as many of the Synod fathers as it could. Some copies were hand-delivered to bishops staying at the St. Martha residence, while others were mailed to apartments in Rome or to the seminaries and other residences where participants were known to be lodging. But there were still scores of bishops whose temporary addresses the publisher could not find.

Father Fessio's team eventually decided to mail a book to each participating bishop in care of the Synod office. Dropped at an Italian post office in Rome, the packages were relayed (none too quickly, as is typical of Italian mail service) to the Vatican's own post office. Some of the bulky envelopes made their way into the temporary mailboxes that had been set up for the Synod participants. Then, mysteriously, they disappeared.

In his book *The Rigging of a Vatican Synod*, Edward Pentin does his best to provide an account of the books' movements. Details proved to be elusive, but two facts emerged. First, when the flood of books arrived, the Vatican post office delivered many—perhaps all—of them without having affixed an official postmark. Second, the secretary general of the Synod office, Cardinal Baldisseri, learned what the envelopes contained and was reportedly furious. The packages seem to have been returned to the Vatican post office to be stamped properly, and some of them may have found their way back into the bishops' Vatican mailboxes more than a week later, when the Synod discussions were already advanced. Many bishops, however, reported that they never received a copy. Suspicious souls theorized that if the books had finally been delivered, they had then been removed from the bishops' mailboxes.

Father Federico Lombardi rejected such conspiracy theories. The books had been delivered, he told reporters; indeed some bishops reported having received more than one copy. (That was undoubtedly true. In their zeal to ensure that the books reached the Synod partici-pants, the publisher's team had used all available addresses and in some cases had more than one address for a particular bishop.) Cardinal Baldisseri, while complaining that the distribution of the book was an attempt to influence the Synod discussions, denied that his office had made any attempt to intercept the books. To be sure, *Remaining in the Truth of Christ* was published with the goal of advancing the debate. But the editor and publisher hoped to influence the debate by presenting persuasive arguments, not by limiting the flow of information to the Synod fathers.

Complaints that the organizers of the Synod were involved in their own attempts to influence the outcome became more frequent as the days passed. During one particularly contentious discussion, the imposing Cardinal George Pell reportedly slammed his hand down on a table and exclaimed, "You must stop manipulating this Synod!"

Interim Report Sparks Angry Reactions

Controversy at the Synod intensified on October 13 with the release of an interim report—the *relatio post disceptationem*—which was supposed to summarize the first week's discussions and serve as the basis for the second week's deliberations. Many participants, however, thought the *relatio* misrepresented their views. The next day the Vatican press office announced defensively that "a value has been attributed to the document that does not correspond to its nature," emphasizing that it was merely "a working document."

At the news conference introducing the *relatio*, reporters were openly skeptical about some of the more controversial passages of the document. When questioned about the statement that homosexuals "have gifts and qualities to offer to the Christian community," Archbishop Bruno Forte, who drafted that section, gave an answer that "played to decidedly mixed reviews both inside and outside the Synod hall," reported John Allen of *Crux*.

Cardinal Burke charged that the *relatio* "advances positions which many Synod Fathers do not accept and, I would say, as faithful shepherds of the flock cannot accept," and Cardinal Pell described it as a "tendentious, skewed" account. Among the bishops with whom Pell had discussed the *relatio*, he said, fully three-quarters were unsatisfied with it.

When the South African cardinal Wilfrid Napier was asked whether the bishops approved of the *relatio*, he remarked that they had no opportunity to do so. The document had been released to the press before it was presented to the Synod fathers. This was an important tactical point, because first impressions are lasting. The reporters covering the Synod, anxious for solid news about the deliberations, would pounce on this first document and broadcast it worldwide. Any subsequent statements from the Synod would be read in the light of this interim report. So the staff of the Synod had succeeded in setting the terms of the public debate, if not the bishops' discussions.

Cardinal Péter Erdő of Hungary, who as relator general was responsible, on paper, for the preparation of the *relatio*, made no special effort to conceal that substantial portions of the document had been prepared without his involvement. Pope Francis himself, who had frequently spoken about the importance of synodal government in the Church, was a party to this subversion of the assembly's procedures, having appointed the officials running the Synod office and having approved their decision to release the interim report to the press before presenting it to the Synod fathers.

Archbishop Stanisław Gadecki, the president of the Polish bishops' conference, told Vatican Radio that the *relatio* failed to provide solid support for "good, normal, ordinary families" striving to fulfill the Christian ideal of marriage. "It is not so much what the document says but what it does not say that has been noticed," the archbishop lamented. "It focuses on exceptions, but what is needed is the proclamation of truth."

Many prelates observed that the early release of the *relatio* had triggered an enormous volume of media coverage, much of it inaccurate, conveying the impression that the Church would change her teachings. The BBC, for example, announced that Francis had "scored a first quiet victory," convincing "many Catholic Church leaders to moderate their formerly strongly critical language about gay unions."

A "Virtually Irredeemable" Position

"We're now working from a position that's virtually irredeemable," said Cardinal Napier, referring to the media coverage. "The message has gone out that this is what the Synod is saying, that this is what the Catholic Church is saying," he said. "Whatever we say hereafter will seem like we're doing damage control."

Among their many objections to the *relatio*, critics frequently cited the document's failure to incorporate the thought of St. John Paul II, whose "theology of the body" was one of the most important magisterial developments since the Second Vatican Council. It would have seemed appropriate, then, for a new statement by the Synod to build on that foundation. Instead the document largely ignored John Paul's work.

The Kasper proposal, in particular, directly contradicted the teaching of John Paul II. In section 84 of his own apostolic exhortation on marriage and family life, *Familiaris Consortio*, issued in 1981, John Paul had written that

> the Church reaffirms her practice, which is based upon Sacred Scripture, of not admitting to Eucharistic Communion divorced persons who have remarried. They are unable to be admitted thereto from the fact that their state and condition of life objectively contradict that union of love between Christ and the Church which is signified and effected by the Eucharist. Besides this, there is another special pastoral reason: if these people were admitted to the Eucharist, the faithful would be led into error and confusion regarding the Church's teaching about the indissolubility of marriage.
>
> Reconciliation in the sacrament of Penance, which would open the way to the Eucharist, can only be granted to those who, repenting of having broken the sign of the Covenant and of fidelity to Christ, are sincerely ready to undertake a way of life that is no longer in contradiction to the indissolubility of marriage.

With a week remaining in the session, the critics of the *relatio* organized a strong campaign to ensure that the Synod's final document would be very different from the interim report. After an opening week in which every bishop had the opportunity to address the whole assembly, the participants were divided into ten working groups, organized by language, for the remainder of the assembly. Cardinal Baldisseri originally announced that the reports of the working groups would not be made public. According to Marco Tosatti of *La Stampa*, that announcement provoked a vigorous protest by Cardinal Erdő. When other prelates joined him, the decision was reversed.

The working groups expressed surprise that the preliminary report had been made public, and most of them registered serious reservations about its contents. Speaking for one of the French-language groups, Cardinal Robert Sarah said that he felt obliged to give voice to the "emotion and confusion provoked by the publication of a document that we considered as a simple (although quite useful) working document, and thus provisional." Cardinal George Pell told the British Catholic journal *The Tablet* that about three-quarters of the Synod fathers had criticized the *relatio*, which he himself described as "tendentious and incomplete." As did many of his brother bishops, he found it "strange that there was so little in the document on scriptural teaching and magisterial teaching on marriage, sexuality, family." Cardinal Müller declared the document "completely wrong" in its portrayal of the Synod fathers' discussion and found it "shameful" that the report had suppressed some points of view while promoting others.

In particular, the working groups complained that the *relatio* had failed to express a positive vision of the Christian understanding of marriage and family life and called for a stronger affirmation of the Church's teaching on marriage and sexuality. The *relatio*, they observed, focused on problematical situations, such as cohabitation, same-sex unions, and divorce. Without ignoring those problems, the reports suggested that the Synod's final statement should "contain a strong message of encouragement and support for the Church and for faithful married couples."

The groups applauded the effort in the *relatio* to depict the Church as a place of welcome for all people, regardless of their difficulties. But the Synod fathers, the Vatican press office reported, feared the document "could give the impression of a willingness on the part of the Church to legitimize irregular family situations," and most of the groups questioned the wisdom of "gradualism" as a pastoral approach to people in irregular unions. An Italian-language group, led by Cardinal Angelo Bagnasco, the archbishop of Genoa, was more sharply critical, saying that the preliminary report "seems to be afraid to express an opinion on several issues that have now become the dominant cultural expressions."

The working groups' reports did not reveal a consensus in favor of allowing divorced and remarried Catholics to receive Communion. Most groups, however, did find broad agreement that if possible, the procedures for obtaining a decree of nullity should be streamlined.

As far as outsiders could tell, the first ten days of the Synod's meeting were focused divorce and remarriage. Much less had been heard about healthy families and still less about the need to promote the teachings of the Catholic Church on the sanctity and indissolubility of marriage. To be fair, the *relatio post disceptationem* did devote some attention to the challenge of evangelizing persons whose lives are at odds with the Christian vision of marriage and family life—gradually drawing them along, helping them to perceive the truth. But that interim document still focused on problems rather than solutions.

Equally important, the *relatio* conveyed the impression to the general public that the Catholic Church was preparing to accept irregular living arrangements that had hitherto been regarded as sinful. As that message spread, it would become increasingly difficult to proclaim the truth about human sexuality. The first words out of the Synod, therefore, were a setback for evangelization.

The Heavy Influence of a Declining German Church

The two previous popes, John Paul II and Benedict XVI, spoke frequently about the "new evangelization"—the effort to revive the Faith in those societies where Christianity was once dominant but has now faded. For the most part, that means Europe and North America, where the Church has suffered sharp declines in Mass attendance, in vocations to the priesthood and religious life, in church weddings, in baptisms.

But if you had to identify the one country in the West where the decline of the Catholic Church is most pronounced, you would probably point to Germany, where a massive exodus testifies to the German Church's evangelical slumber. Each year more than one hundred thousand Germans formally drop their registration in the Catholic Church—to say nothing of the many others who simply stop attending Mass. More than three thousand parishes have been closed in the past decade, while the number of annual baptisms has fallen by roughly one hundred thousand.

Why, then, was the agenda of the extraordinary session of the Synod of Bishops—the theme of which was the family *in the context of evangelization*—dominated by Germans? Cardinal Kasper had introduced the proposal to allow divorced and remarried Catholics to receive Communion. Cardinal Marx, the president of the German bishops' conference, had testified that the Kasper proposal had the full support of the other German bishops. The American Catholic commentator Amy Welborn asked the right question:

> Well, first you should be wondering why the head of a national church that is dying should have this constantly turned-on microphone on this issue. Why are we even listening to him? Aren't we supposed to be listening to the Church from places where it is actually alive and growing?

Where is the Church growing? Most conspicuously in Africa. One might even say that in the early twenty-first century, Africa itself *is* "the context of evangelization." So a Synod dedicated to the family might profitably discuss the difficulties facing Christian families in Africa. And there are many: the lingering influence of pagan customs, polygamy, staged and arranged marriages, poverty, lack of access to health care and education, civil wars, foreign aid that comes tied to anti-family ideology, and, last but not least, Islamic extremism and religious persecution. These are real problems, touching the lives of millions of people. But they were scarcely mentioned in public discussions of the Synod's agenda. Instead, the Western world concentrated on its own favorite problem: the discomfort of those relatively few Catholics who, having divorced and remarried, now wish to receive Communion. At a time when hundreds of thousands of parents are struggling to save their children from starvation or to find new homes where they will be safe from violence, how does one justify putting the Kasper proposal at the top of the agenda? And a more difficult question is how would resolving the situation of these divorced and remarried Catholics ignite a new burst of evangelization?

Ironically enough, the African Church did become the focus of public attention during the second week of the Synod meeting, but not because the bishops were discussing the troubles of African families. Cardinal Kasper was caught disparaging the African bishops, who were resisting his proposal. "They should not tell us too much what we have to do," he complained to a group of journalists. He added that the Africans also blocked a discussion of how the Church might reach out to same-sex couples. Homosexuality is not even mentioned in African societies, the enlightened German observed. "It's a taboo."

At first Kasper denied making these dismissive remarks, whose patronizing tone hinted at racial bias. Then the English journalist who had revealed his comments, Edward Pentin, produced a recording of his exchange with the cardinal. Kasper responded that the interview was unauthorized, but in the recording Pentin clearly identifies himself as a reporter before asking questions. Finally Kasper complained that he had been speaking off the record. That last line of defense soon crumbled as well. He had been speaking with three reporters, and he never said that his remarks were off the record. Kasper was not new to this game; he had dealt with the media, quite skillfully, for years. He certainly knew that comments made to reporters are presumed to be on the record unless the speaker indicates otherwise.

So why would the cardinal have made such remarkably impolitic comments? And why did he imagine that they would not come to light? It seems that he was acquainted with the other two reporters, but not with Pentin. Apparently he was confident (rightly, as it turned out) that the two reporters he knew shared his views and would not publicize his disparaging comments about the African bishops. In other words he thought he was talking with allies rather than with neutral observers.

Adept politicians know how to court the media, offering reporters an exclusive interview here, a bit of inside information there, a background briefing now and then. Kasper had been making the rounds for months, shoring support for his initiative. He had worked the press well; it was not by chance that the media coverage for his proposal was overwhelmingly favorable. But now he was the victim of his own success. He had been profoundly embarrassed because he made the assumption that Pentin, like so many other reporters, was playing for his team.

Finally, even if the cardinal had said that he was speaking off the record (which he did not), and even if Pentin had been acting unethically when he recorded the conversation (which he was not), the fact remained that *Kasper did make those dismissive comments* about the concerns of some fellow bishops. He left no doubt that he viewed the Synod as an opportunity to address First World problems and saw the African bishops as a hindrance.

An Early Bid for Acceptance of Homosexuality

In those unguarded comments, Cardinal Kasper brought up homosexuality, expressing his dissatisfaction that the Synod had not spent more time on that topic. By all accounts, in fact, very little had been said about homosexuality during the bishops' deliberations. Father Lombardi told reporters that of the 250 or so talks during the plenary sessions, only one address focused on homosexuality.

Nevertheless, no fewer than four paragraphs on pastoral care for homosexuals appeared in the interim report. The Associated Press reported that these paragraphs had been drafted by Archbishop Bruno Forte, the secretary of the committee appointed by the pope to draft the *relatio*, and at the press conference introducing the *relatio*, Cardinal Erdő seemed to confirm Forte's authorship of those paragraphs by referring all questions about homosexuality to him.

Forte evidently introduced his own thoughts into a report that was intended to summarize the ideas expressed by Synod fathers. When the *relatio* was read aloud, Forte and the Italian Jesuit Antonio Spadaro exchanged a very visible thumbs-up sign. Robert Royal observed, "This seems to suggest that not even they were certain … that those passages would survive into the interim document."

A few insiders, then, were able to slip their personal ideas into a document that was intended to summarize the thoughts of the Synod fathers. The gratuitous reference to homosexuality was one more piece of evidence that the Synod's organizers were doing their utmost to control the gathering and its message.

Cardinal Sarah, the prefect of the Congregation for Divine Worship, minced no words in denouncing this manipulation of the Synod message. In a briefing with reporters, he said that "what has been published by the media about homosexual unions is an attempt to push the Church [to change] her doctrine." Such reports were inaccurate, he said: "The Church has never judged homosexual persons, but homosexual behavior and homosexual unions are grave deviations of sexuality."

Sarah also called attention to the strong statement in the Synod's interim report that the Catholic Church cannot accept "gender theory." A native of Guinea, Sarah related that several African prelates had decried the common Western practice of making foreign aid contingent on developing nations' acceptance of gender theory and other anti-family ideologies. This problem, he suggested, deserves wider attention.

Cardinal Pell also wanted to dispel the notion that the Synod would advocate radical change in Church teaching on marriage. "We're not giving in to the secular agenda; we're not collapsing in a heap," he insisted. "We've got no intention of following those radical elements in all the Christian churches, according to the Catholic churches in one or two countries, and going out of business." The Australian added a pointed observation about the motives of those pushing for change:

> Communion for the divorced and remarried is for some—very few, certainly not the majority of synod fathers—it's only the tip of the iceberg, it's a stalking horse. They want wider changes, recognition of civil unions, recognition of homosexual unions.

An Inconclusive Final Document

After the stormy introduction of the *relatio* and the heated complaints about the manipulation of the message, the October 2014 meeting moved toward a relatively quiet conclusion, the bishops approving a final message that expressed appreciation for families and highlighted the struggles they face. Family life, the message stated, is "a mountainous trek with hardships and falls. God is always there to accompany us." Unlike the controversial *relatio*, the final report included many references to Sacred Scripture and documents of the Magisterium.

The Synod fathers had the opportunity to vote on each of the report's sixty-two paragraphs, and the press office published the vote tallies for each paragraph. For example, paragraph 56, which stated that it is "totally unacceptable" that aid to poor nations be contingent upon legalization of same-sex marriage, passed by a 159-21 margin.

Every paragraph in the final report received a majority vote, but three paragraphs failed to receive the required two-thirds supermajority. Paragraphs 52 and 53 stated that the Synod fathers disagreed about admitting remarried persons to Communion and that the issue required further study. Paragraph 55 stated that some families have persons with a homosexual orientation, that they are to be accepted with respect and sensitivity, and that same-sex unions are not remotely similar to marriage.

Cardinal Burke called the final document "a significant improvement" over the interim report. "I would say that it provides an accurate, if not complete, summary of the discussions in the Synod Hall and in the small groups," he told *Catholic World Report*. "It is a blow to those who wrote the material which did not reflect the Church's teaching regarding the homosexual condition and homosexual acts, which implied that the Church wants now to relax its perennial teaching, and which tried to introduce material regarding so-called 'same-sex unions' into the discussion of Christian marriage."

In his concluding address to the Synod, the pope compared the two-week meeting to an arduous journey. Since it was "a journey of human beings, with the consolations there were also moments of desolation, of tensions and temptations, of which a few possibilities could be mentioned."

In mentioning those "possibilities," the pope carefully balanced his remarks, warning "traditionalists" against "a temptation to hostile inflexibility" and "progressives and liberals" against a temptation to "a deceptive mercy that binds the wounds without first curing them." He warned against "the temptation to neglect the 'depositum fidei' [the deposit of faith]" and "the temptation to neglect reality, making use of meticulous language and a language of smoothing to say so many things and to say nothing!"

The final document of the 2014 Synod meeting received nowhere near the attention that the more radical *relatio* did. The earlier document, suggesting a major change in Church teaching, had admittedly been more newsworthy. But in the English-speaking world there was another reason why the preliminary report drew more attention. The official English translation of the bishops' final document was not available until ten days after the Synod closed, when the bishops had gone home and the reporters covering the event had moved on to other subjects.

Even then, the English translation had its defects, including one blatant omission. The bishops' final statement, issued in Italian, noted that the Synod fathers came together to "discern how the Church and society can renew their commitment to the family *founded on marriage between a man and a woman*." Those italicized words were omitted from the Vatican's official English translation. No one who had witnessed the manipulation of the 2014 Synod meeting was likely to think that the omission was accidental.

CHAPTER FIVE

The Unanswered Question

The ordinary assembly of the Synod of Bishops that convened in October 2015 was mostly a reprise of the extraordinary assembly of a year earlier. The topic was the same—marriage and the family—and the same arguments were rehearsed, the same tensions exposed. But there were two important differences. First, complaints about manipulation of the proceedings subsided, perhaps because bishops were on the alert, ready to object to any suspicious stratagems. Second, and more important, this session would produce a final report that would in turn form the basis for an important magisterial document by Pope Francis.

As a Synod meeting concludes, the bishops vote on a series of propositions. Those that are approved by a two-thirds majority constitute the final report of the Synod. But since the Synod is an advisory body, its report is not the last word. Rather, the pope summarizes the results of the discussion in an "apostolic exhortation," an expression of the papal magisterium that carries a high (though not the highest) level of authority.

At the 2014 meeting of the Synod, Francis had given many indications of his leanings but had not openly sided with the proponents of change. Although he had expressed his enthusiasm for Cardinal

Kasper's work, he had not endorsed the proposal to allow Communion for divorced-and-remarried Catholics. While he had appointed the officials who organized the meeting, he had not been directly involved in their shenanigans. So it was still possible to believe that the pope would accept the outcome of the bishops' deliberations on the issue that had come to dominate the discussion.

There had been some early signs, to be sure, that the pope would side with Kasper, to whom he had given the floor at the consistory of cardinals in February 2014. Then a few months later there were reports that the pope himself had advised a woman that she should receive Communion despite her divorce and remarriage.

In April 2014 the Vatican confirmed that the pope had placed one of his surprise telephone calls to a woman in Argentina, Jaquelina Lisbona, who had written to him about her marital situation, pleading for permission to receive the Eucharist. Lisbona—who professed dismay at the international attention given to the story—told an Argentine radio station that while *she* is not divorced, her husband, Julio Sabetta, *is* divorced and remarried. Because their marriage is not recognized by the Church, Lisbona said, her pastor had told her that she is barred from the Sacraments.

After the pope called her, Lisbona's husband wrote on his Facebook page that the pontiff had told his wife "that she should go to confession and start taking Communion at a different parish." In his second-hand account of the conversation, Sabetta claimed that the pope had assured his wife that "a divorced person who goes to Communion is not doing anything wrong." (To be sure, the Church allows divorced Catholics to receive Communion—provided that they do not attempt a second marriage.)

The Vatican press office indicated that it would not comment on the pope's telephone call, emphasizing that reports about that conversation "cannot be confirmed as reliable." In any case, the statement continued, the pope's advice to an individual could not be regarded as a statement of Church teaching, since such conversations would "not

in any way form part of the Pope's public activities." The Vatican statement added that "consequences relating to the teaching of the Church
are not to be inferred from these occurrences."

Still the pope's telephone conversation raised disturbing questions.
Did he really dispense pastoral advice—in a case that he could not
possibly have known well—over an international telephone line? Did
he really tell a woman that she should receive Communion in spite of
her involvement in a marriage that the Church could not sanction?
While a prudent reader might ordinarily question the accuracy of such
an account, Francis had made so many unexpected phone calls and
unconventional statements that this conversation, as reported, seemed
quite plausible.

Questions about the pope's thinking swirled around the preparations for the second Synod session, feeding suspicions that he was
determined to secure the bishops' approval of the Kasper proposal. The
speculation was heightened when the pope invoked the "principles of
gradualness," language that some had employed to justify a change in
Church teaching. John Paul II had used that term in 1981 in his own
apostolic exhortation *Familiaris Consortio*. Acknowledging that many
people will make only gradual progress toward a life of virtue, the Polish pope had nevertheless clearly indicated that pastors should *not* shy
away from a clear statement of Church teachings:

> They cannot however look on the law as merely an ideal to
> be achieved in the future: they must consider it as a com-
> mand of Christ the Lord to overcome difficulties with con-
> stancy. And so what is known as "the law of gradualness" or
> step-by-step advance cannot be identified with "gradualness
> of the law," as if there were different degrees or forms of
> precept in God's law for different individuals and situations.

If "gradualness" means "meeting people where they are" and opening a conversation that might lead them to Christ, then it is not only a

prudent approach but a pastoral necessity. But advocates for the Kasper proposal seemed to suggest something different: a willingness to tolerate sin, to pretend that a wound is a sign of health. Father Vincent Twomey, a prominent Irish theologian who studied for his doctorate under Joseph Ratzinger, has remarked that this approach is neither bold nor properly pastoral: "There is nothing very courageous about offering 'pastoral' recommendations that fail to challenge a world that still bears the scars of the sexual revolution of the 1960s."

Streamlined Annulment Procedures

Even before the Synod fathers convened in October 2015 for their second round of discussions on the family, it seemed possible that the pope might take the most contentious issue—the Kasper proposal—off the table by making it easier to obtain a decree of nullity.

Some Catholic couples whose unions have broken down have never been truly married in the eyes of the Church. A canonical decree acknowledging that their supposed marriage is not valid leaves them free to remarry (or, in the eyes of the Church, to marry for a first time) and still to receive Communion. If marriage tribunals operated as efficiently as one might wish, granting relief promptly and without burdensome expense to those who qualified, then the Kasper proposal might be moot.

Early in September, just a few weeks before the Synod met, Francis announced changes to the Code of Canon Law streamlining the procedure for annulments. He explained that he was motivated by the desire to help those Catholics who "are too often separated from the legal structures of the churches due to physical or moral distance" and recalled that such reforms were frequently mentioned during the October 2014 discussions of the Synod.

These reforms, the pope emphasized, do not alter the Church's clear teaching on the indissolubility of marriage. The canonical changes, he noted, are "provisions that favor not the nullity of marriage but rather the speed of processes, along with the appropriate simplicity, so that the heart of the faithful who await clarification of their status is not long oppressed by the darkness of doubt due to the lengthy wait for a conclusion."

The principal reforms were:

- The elimination of fees for annulment petitions. The costs were now to be borne by the diocese.
- The elimination of a mandatory review for every judgment of nullity. The "moral certainty reached by the first judge according to law should be sufficient."
- The option for having cases heard by a single judge appointed by the bishop, rather than a court of three judges.
- An accelerated process for cases in which the evidence appears clear that a sacramental marriage never took place.

These changes, which took effect in December 2015, would have little practical effect on Catholics in the United States, the country that accounts for nearly half of the annulments handed down by Church tribunals worldwide. Though the new "fast-track" option would benefit those who qualified for it, most American Catholics already had easy access to marriage tribunals, and many dioceses had already waived the fees associated with a petition for annulment. Nevertheless, the reforms were expected to affect the discussions of the Synod. As John Allen predicted,

> The decision will recalibrate the discussion at October's second edition of the Synod of Bishops on the family, likely reducing the emphasis on the question of Communion for divorced and remarried Catholics and creating space for other issues to emerge.

The streamlined annulment procedure eliminated one argument for the Kasper proposal—namely, that many Catholics, particularly in impoverished dioceses, did not have access to marriage tribunals. The reforms also responded to the call, originally made by Benedict XVI, for more ways to bring the divorced and remarried back into active involvement in Church life.

An annulment is not a favor granted by Church officials. A "declaration of nullity," as it is properly called, is a juridical finding that a particular union has never been a valid marriage. If there is no marriage, then as a matter of justice the Church should reach that verdict as quickly as practicable so the man and woman know they are free to enter new unions.

Unfortunately, as the Synod fathers observed, in many parts of the world Catholics do not have ready access to marriage tribunals. Even where tribunals operate with reasonable efficiency, the process can be cumbersome and costly. So an easy consensus emerged from the previous Synod sessions that the annulment process should be streamlined.

Now Francis had swept away those difficulties. The process had been simplified, and the costs (to petitioners) had been eliminated. In cases where there were obvious grounds for annulment, the diocesan bishop could quickly issue a verdict. Once the papal reforms were in place, it should be easy—too easy, critics feared—for Catholic couples to obtain a declaration of nullity.

With their first unions annulled and their new marriages regularized, thousands of Catholic couples would be welcome to receive the Eucharist. So who would be left as potential beneficiaries of the Kasper proposal? Only those who could *not* receive annulments because they *were* truly married the first time. And it seemed clearly impossible to accept those couples back into the full sacramental life of the Church—and thus to accept their second unions—without rejecting the words of Jesus.

October 4—the opening day of the 2015 Synod meeting—was the twenty-seventh Sunday of Ordinary Time in the Church's liturgical calendar. The Gospel that Catholics all around the world heard proclaimed at Mass that day, taken from the tenth chapter of St. Mark, seemed uncannily apt:

And Pharisees came up and in order to test him asked, "Is it lawful for a man to divorce his wife?"

He answered them, "What did Moses command you?"

They said, "Moses allowed a man to write a certificate of divorce, and to put her away."

But Jesus said to them, "For your hardness of heart he wrote you this commandment.

"But from the beginning of creation, 'God made them male and female.'

'For this reason a man shall leave his father and mother and be joined to his wife, and the two shall become one flesh.' So they are no longer two but one flesh.

"What therefore God has joined together, let not man put asunder."

And in the house the disciples asked him again about this matter.

And he said to them, "Whoever divorces his wife and marries another, commits adultery against her; and if she divorces her husband and marries another, she commits adultery."

Demonizing the Critics

When the Synod opened its deliberations, acrimony was aired less freely than in the earlier session but it was still felt. The pope renewed his call for free and open debate, but liberal Catholic pundits hinted that anyone who opposed the Kasper proposal was defying the pontiff. The German-speaking bishops issued assurances that no one contemplated a change in Church teaching, but when conservatives said that the Church *must* not change her teaching, they were denounced as "Pharisees"—one of the strongest epithets in the progressive churchman's lexicon. Vatican spokesmen dismissed "conspiracy theories" about manipulation of the Synod, but bishops who argued against potentially revolutionary changes were charged with forming a cabal. The most unseemly aspect of the 2015 Synod meeting was not the lively argument but the aggressive effort by a cadre of ideologues to depict their opponents as villains.

Yes, there were some serious differences of opinion among the bishops gathered in Rome that October. That was to be expected. Some major changes in Church teaching had been suggested; it would have been unhealthy if such proposals did *not* prompt vigorous debate. The purpose of the Synod was to hash out ideas. Even without the pope's repeated encouragement, some level of disagreement among the bishops would have been inevitable. If there were no differences among them, the bishops could have stayed home.

Naturally, prelates who had strong opinions did their best to convince others. Bishops made alliances with others who shared their views and tried to bring their undecided brethren on board. Again, there was nothing unusual about that. As Archbishop Charles Chaput of Philadelphia observed, "I have never been at a Church meeting where there aren't groups that get together and lobby for a particular direction."

What *was* extraordinary about this Synod meeting was a two-pronged effort to curb open discussion: first by manipulating the Synod (as recounted in the previous chapter), and second by silencing those who dared to report on the manipulation.

In its daily briefings on the Synod's progress, the Vatican press office relied on prelates who would provide an upbeat account. Cardinal Péter Erdő, the relator general for the Synod—the official appointed by the pope to summarize the discussion—was in the best position to summarize the discussions for the press, but after delivering a strongly conservative address on the opening day, he virtually disappeared from view.

It was not surprising that the Vatican press office wanted to ensure that the Synod's discussions were presented to the public in a favorable light. What was remarkable was that a press office aide—Father Thomas Rosica, a Canadian who helped with English-language media—emerged as an active partisan, sending out messages from liberal prelates and commentators on his Twitter account. Still more remarkable, Rosica, who as a public-relations man should have been looking for the widest possible audience, began blocking conservatives from his Twitter feed. As the Synod debate heated up, he passed along advice on "How to handle toxic people," demonstrating that while liberal Catholics didn't want anyone excluded from the Church, they would gladly exclude some people from the conversation.

Still more troubling was the polemical tone adopted by Father Antonio Spadaro, the editor of *La Civiltà Cattolica*, a Jesuit journal whose articles are approved before publication by the Secretariat of State. A papal confidant and occasional ghost-writer who has been called "the pope's mouthpiece," he worked closely with Francis throughout the Synod process. In light of his close ties with the pontiff, one might have expected Spadaro to adopt an irenic approach to the Synod debates, but he poured out barbs on his Twitter feed with Trumpian abandon, mocking those who questioned the apparent direction of the Synod. On October 10 he tweeted, "The Church isn't a fast train of doctrine which runs without any understanding of the landscape around it"—a statement that is at best cryptic and at worst incoherent. Later in the day he took a more explicitly adversarial stand: "Those who want a rigid & mummified #Synod15 are attacking its method & communication."

Father James Martin, a high-profile American Jesuit, joined the campaign with a series of tweets praising liberal prelates and criticizing conservatives. He reached his own peak of partisanship with the assertion that Cardinal Robert Sarah had compared homosexuals to Nazis, a grossly unfair characterization of the cardinal's remarks about the dangers of gender ideology.

Yet another Jesuit, the journalist Thomas Reese, was equally unsubtle in his summary of the Synod debate: "One side sees only the law—the marriage contract is permanent and can be terminated only by death. The other side sees millions of people suffering from broken marriages that cannot be put back together." And responding to complaints that the Synod was being railroaded, he spun his own conspiracy theory: "They're saying that it's being manipulated and preprogrammed when, in point of fact, all of the synods since the Second Vatican Council were manipulated and programmed but by the conservatives."

This partisan tone eventually affected the Synod participants themselves. Cardinal Donald Wuerl of Washington, D.C., in an interview with the Jesuit magazine *America*, spoke disparagingly about "some bishops whose position is that we shouldn't be discussing any of this anyway" and who "paint something in false tones." He wondered "if it is really that they find they just don't like the Pope."

Such was the atmosphere in which the pope himself, on October 7, delivered an unscheduled address to the Synod in which, according to multiple reports, he admonished the prelates against indulging in conspiracy theories.

Cardinals Plead for Open Debate

Shortly after that papal intervention, Sandro Magister, the veteran Vatican-watcher for *L'Espresso*, published a letter to Francis, dated October 5 and signed by thirteen cardinals, expressing serious concerns about the conduct of the Synod. The letter's existence, its contents, and the names of its signers quickly became the dominant topic of discussion at the Vatican.

After expressing misgivings about the Synod's working document, as well as the procedures and the composition of the committee that would draft the final document, the signatories wrote:

In turn, these things have created a concern that the new procedures are not true to the traditional spirit and purpose of a synod. It is unclear why these procedural changes are necessary. A number of fathers feel the new process seems designed to facilitate predetermined results on important disputed questions.

Finally and perhaps most urgently, various fathers have expressed concern that a synod designed to address a vital pastoral matter—reinforcing the dignity of marriage and family—may become dominated by the theological/doctrinal issue of Communion for the divorced and civilly remarried. If so, this will inevitably raise even more fundamental issues about how the Church, going forward, should interpret and apply the Word of God, her doctrines and her disciplines to changes in culture. The collapse of liberal Protestant churches in the modern era, accelerated by their abandonment of key elements of Christian belief and practice in the name of pastoral adaptation, warrants great caution in our own synodal discussions.

The signers, according to Magister, were Cardinals Carlo Caffarra, Thomas Collins, Timothy Dolan, Willem Eijk, Péter Erdő, Gerhard Müller, Wilfrid Napier, George Pell, Mauro Piacenza, Robert Sarah, Angelo Scola, Jorge Urosa Savino, and André Vingt-Trois. That list of signatories was impressive. Cardinal Erdő was the synod's relator general, while Napier and Vingt-Trois were among the synod's four presidents-delegate. Müller, Pell, and Piacenza headed offices of the Roman Curia.

Some of the cardinals on that list, however, denied having signed the letter. It was not clear how Magister obtained the letter or why he listed the names of cardinals who now said they had not signed it. Informed Vatican sources indicated that a letter had indeed been

written, but Magister's information regarding the letter and its signatories was imprecise. Many Vatican-watchers speculated that Francis
was responding to this letter when, in his October 7 address to the
Synod, he reportedly cautioned against applying a "hermeneutic of
conspiracy" to the procedures for the meeting.

And who had leaked the cardinals' letter? Ordinarily, in searching
for the source of a leaked document, the first order of business is to
consider whose interests would be served by the publicity. In this case,
however, it was not at all clear who would benefit from the publication
of a confidential letter to the pope.

At first glance it might seem that the authors of the letter had the
most to gain. If they were not satisfied with the response they received
from the Holy Father, they might want to add some public pressure for
their cause. Two considerations support that hypothesis. First, the leak
came through Magister, who had frequently been critical of Francis
and had raised questions in his own columns similar to those raised
by the cardinals' letter. Second, the letter became public only after
Francis responded to the cardinals' concerns—a week or more after it
had been written.

Nevertheless, the publication of a confidential letter may have
damaged the cause of the cardinals who wrote it. The leak was perceived as an underhanded attempt to manipulate public opinion—in
short, an act of disloyalty. Cardinal Müller, who refused to confirm or
deny that he had signed the letter, was steaming over the leak, saying
that it created the appearance that Francis was surrounded by "wolves"
who sought to undermine his authority. So perhaps the leak was
intended to make trouble for the cardinals who signed the letter.

Speculation aside, the public release of the letter *did* seem to serve
the interests of the journalist Sandro Magister. This was not his first
important leak. The previous June, the Vatican press office had suspended his press privileges after he published an early draft of the papal
encyclical *Laudato Si'*. The Vatican had stressed that the draft published

by Magister was not the final text, but there were no significant differences between the two. He did not have the final document, but he had something very close.

Likewise, Magister had not gotten his hands on the final text of the cardinals' letter to Francis. Cardinal Pell—who acknowledged that he had signed the letter—reported that Magister's version contained "errors in both the content and the list of signatories." But as Magister would later point out, Pell did not deny that the concerns expressed in the final draft were essentially the same as those in Magister's version. It seems likely, then, that after Magister obtained a draft that was circulating among a number of cardinals, the letter was eventually revised and signed by a somewhat different group.

Cardinal Urosa, who acknowledged signing the letter, said that "many cardinals" had seen it, either in draft or final form. If multiple copies were circulating, then it is not surprising that one found its way into the hands of a journalist. What is noteworthy, actually, is Magister's failure to obtain the final version. It suggests that the cardinals who signed the letter were not eager to publicize it and, more important, that they did not leak it after it was delivered to the pope and he had responded to them.

The available evidence, in short, does not allow us to identify the leaker, let alone his motivation. But this much we do know: once again, on the basis of a leaked document, the Vatican was caught up in an unhealthy welter of accusations and denials. Once again, *someone* at the Vatican was determined to undermine someone else. Once again, the dignity of the Holy See was battered by stories of palace intrigues.

A Final Statement—without a Conclusion

As October drew toward a close, the debates and maneuvers and leaks and complaints came to an end, and the Synod fathers approved their final set of propositions. In separate interviews following the conclusion of the meeting, Archbishop Forte and Cardinal Pell offered contradictory interpretations of the Synod's final judgment about the Kasper proposal.

Pell told the *National Catholic Register* that "there is no mention anywhere of Communion for the divorced and remarried. It's not one of the possibilities that was floated." Yet Forte, the synod's special secretary, told a radio audience that the final report permits the reception of Holy Communion by "some" persons who have remarried outside the Church, following an examination of conscience and a discernment process with their pastors.

Was the report really that ambiguous? With his usual candor, Pell said that it was not so much ambiguous as "insufficient"—and deliberately so. He told the *Register*: "The document is cleverly written to get consensus."

Thanks to some careful phrasing, the Synod had achieved consensus—barely. Paragraph 86, which encourages divorced and remarried Catholics to resort to the "internal forum" (conversation with a priest) to discern the obstacles to their "fuller participation in the life of the Church," received just one vote more than the required two-thirds majority. But the Synod did not achieve clarity. The Catholic Church either does or does not hold that couples in a second conjugal relationship whose previous spouses are living should not receive Communion. Which is it? Different prelates gave different answers.

When the Synod of Bishops gathers, the faithful expect to deepen their understanding of what the Church teaches. Admittedly, the Synod does not teach with authority. Only the pope, in his own postsynodal statement, does that. But bishops are teachers, and we have a right to expect instruction rather than confusion or, worse, obfuscation.

During the Synod discussions, there were frequent suggestions that the Church should use more welcoming language, adopt a more compassionate attitude, offer more winsome arguments. Yes, we all want welcoming pastors, compassionate confessors, and winsome evangelists. But from our teachers we want clarity. At this assembly of the Synod, we were told, the bishops were concerned with pastoral matters, not doctrinal issues. Yet the Kasper proposal raised a major doctrinal question, and rather than addressing that question directly, the Synod tried to finesse it.

On questions of doctrine, as on questions of law, precise language is crucial. A lawyer who drafts a contract with deliberately ambiguous language to cover up a lack of agreement between the parties is inviting disaster. Since the Synod's statement was not binding, however, the danger to the Faith could be averted if the pope, fulfilling his God-given duty as the Church's supreme teacher, addressed the question that the Synod fathers avoided.

Catholics who had followed the Synod debate now anxiously awaited Francis's apostolic exhortation. And it was a relatively short wait. John Paul II and Benedict XVI had routinely taken two years to complete their apostolic exhortations after previous assemblies of the Synod. But never before had the Synod left such a crucial question unresolved.

CHAPTER SIX

The Document and the Dubia

In April 2016, Pope Francis issued his apostolic exhortation summarizing the Synod's message. Comprising 325 numbered paragraphs and filling more than 250 pages, *Amoris Laetitia* ("The Joy of Love") is the lengthiest papal document on record. Attributing this length to the "rich fruits of the two-year Synod process" and the "wide variety of questions" raised, the pope advises against "a rushed reading of the text" (7)[1]—advice that the media necessarily ignored in their hurry to announce the papal verdict on the matters that had conspicuously vexed the world's bishops.

Despite its prolixity, *Amoris Laetitia* provides no clear answer to the question that everyone was asking: whether the pope would open the door for divorced-and-remarried Catholics to receive Communion. Some commentators announced that the pope had upheld traditional Church teaching; others declared that he had made a dramatic innovation. Neither interpretation of this puzzling document is demonstrably wrong.

In fact, Francis deliberately avoids a categorical answer to the question, insisting that "not all discussions of doctrinal, moral, or pastoral

---

1 Numbers in parentheses refer to the numbered paragraphs in the quoted document.

issues need to be settled by interventions of the magisterium" (3). He argues that "what is part of a practical discernment in particular circumstances cannot be elevated to the level of a rule" (304), urging pastors to guide couples through a discernment of their situation, helping them to "grow in the life of grace and charity, while receiving the Church's help to this end" (305).

In the passage that comes closest to an endorsement of the Kasper proposal, paragraph 305, Francis teaches that "a pastor cannot feel that it is enough simply to apply moral laws to those living in 'irregular' situations, as if they were stones to throw at people's lives." Pressing further, he writes that "it is possible that in an objective situation of sin—which may not be subjectively culpable, or fully such—a person can be living in God's grace, can love and can also grow in the life of grace and charity, while receiving the Church's help to this end." In the accompanying footnote, number 351, he adds, "In certain cases, this can include the help of the sacraments."

That passage—and especially that footnote—could be read, and indeed *was* read by many interpreters, as adopting the Kasper proposal. Is the pope saying that some Catholics who are living in irregular marital unions may receive the sacraments? Is he suggesting that a second marital union, which the Church has always regarded as adulterous, might be justifiable under special circumstances? If so, he is making a radical change in the teachings of the Church. Yet his actual language leaves these crucial questions unanswered. Apparently that was his intent.

"By thinking that everything is black and white," paragraph 305 continues, "we sometimes close off the way of grace and of growth, and discourage paths of sanctification which give glory to God." Later Francis adds, "I understand those who prefer a more rigorous pastoral care which leaves no room for confusion. But I sincerely believe that Jesus wants a Church attentive to the goodness which the Holy Spirit sows in the midst of human weakness..." (308). *Amoris Laetitia* offers little guidance to the pastors who must provide "the Church's help" to persons in irregular marriages. Emphasizing flexibility, the pope leaves the details to others: "Different communities will have to devise more practical and effective initiatives that respect both the Church's teaching and local problems and needs" (199).

Francis devotes only a small portion of his apostolic exhortation to the question of Communion for divorced-and-remarried Catholics, which he does not take up until paragraph 291. The most important theme of the document, he has declared, is the beauty of marital love, the subject of its "central chapters" (four and five of nine). In a long and deep meditation on St. Paul's ode to love in 1 Corinthians 13 ("Love is patient and kind…"), the pope offers the sort of spiritual wisdom and practical advice that he encourages priests to provide for their people, followed by an explanation of how the family, based on marriage and nourished by the Sacraments, should provide material and moral support not only for its own members, but for its neighbors and society at large.

A proper understanding of marriage and human sexuality, writes Francis, is crucial to restoring health to our troubled society. In the Western world especially, where secular society is often hostile to the Christian ideal of marriage, the Church must uphold that ideal even against public pressure.

Nevertheless, despite this strong reaffirmation of traditional Catholic teaching, *Amoris Laetitia* was introduced to the world as a harbinger of change in the Church's pastoral ministry. At the press conference introducing the apostolic exhortation, Cardinal Christoph Schönborn of Vienna declared, "Something has changed in ecclesial discourse," emphasizing the pope's call for pastoral flexibility.

The focus of public attention on the Church's handling of "irregular" marital unions has itself been a sign of the need for a different approach, Schönborn said, arguing that the division of couples into "regular" and "irregular" overlooks the reality that all Christians should be striving for daily conversion and growth in holiness.

Though Schönborn had been counted as a supporter of the Kasper proposal in the Synod meetings, he did not initially depict *Amoris Laetitia* as an endorsement of that position. (Later he would state that the papal document called for a change in the Church's practice.) He told Vatican Radio that in the critical footnote 351—"In certain cases, this can include the help of the sacraments"—the pope was referring primarily to the sacrament of confession. "I think it is very clear," the cardinal said, "there are circumstances in which people in irregular situations may really need sacramental absolution, even if their general situation cannot be clarified."

The final verdict of the apostolic exhortation on the issue that has been most heavily debated thus remains imprecise. Evidently the pope wishes it so, explaining that "what is part of a practical discernment in particular circumstances cannot be elevated to the level of a rule. That would not only lead to an intolerable casuistry, but would endanger the very values which must be preserved with special care."

Amoris Laetitia is not a revolutionary document. It is a subversive one. Francis has not overthrown the traditional teachings of the Church, as many Catholics hoped or feared that he would. Instead he has carved out ample room for a flexible pastoral interpretation of those teachings, encouraging pastors to help couples apply general moral principles to their specific circumstances. Unfortunately, this approach has accelerated an already powerful trend to dismiss the Church's perennial teaching, eroding respect for the pastoral ministry he hopes to encourage.

In his landmark 1993 encyclical *Veritatis Splendor*, written to counter the influence of moral relativism, St. John Paul II laments the widespread dissent from the Church's moral teachings: "It is no longer a matter of limited and occasional dissent, but of an overall and systematic calling into question of traditional moral doctrines, on the basis of certain anthropological and ethical presuppositions." Dissident Catholics, he explains, are not merely making erroneous statements about the truth; they are suggesting that objective truth cannot be known. *Amoris Laetitia*, focusing on the subjective pursuit of an unreachable ideal and suggesting a process by which Catholic couples could set aside the Lord's commandment against adultery, contributes to the centrifugal forces that are straining the authority of the Church.

In a 250-Page Document, the Focus on a Footnote

There is sound spiritual guidance in *Amoris Laetitia*. Particularly in the two central chapters that the pope himself identifies as its core, he shows his true character as a pastor: encouraging, guiding, questioning, cajoling, sympathizing, instructing, helping readers to gain a deeper appreciation for the Church's understanding of sacramental marriage. He upholds the ideal of Christian marriage, recognizes that no human being lives up to that ideal, and offers the support of the Church to all who are willing to engage in the lifelong struggle to grow in love.

Still, it is noteworthy that Francis emphasizes that the Christian teaching on marriage is an ideal that ordinary couples cannot expect to attain. The Church's teaching is an "ideal," certainly, insofar as it calls husband and wife to live in a perfect harmony of love, in imitation of Christ and his Church. But the demand for marital fidelity is not an unattainable ideal. Most couples meet that demand, and those who do not—those who cheat on their spouses—should recognize that their failure is a serious transgression, not just a reminder that they are human. It is true that Jesus declined to condemn the woman caught in adultery, but he also warned her, "Go, and sin no more" (John 8:11).

In *Amoris Laetitia* the pope recognizes, and clearly states, that the Christian understanding of marriage is the only reliable antidote to a host of ills that plague contemporary society, especially in the West. In the second chapter, he insists that in an epidemic of marital breakdown, Catholics must not be deterred from delivering the message that our society needs to hear, even though that message is unpopular and those who proclaim it face mounting hostility. There are even a few echoes of the "culture wars" in this apostolic exhortation, as Francis unequivocally confirms the Church's stands on abortion, contraception, divorce, homosexuality, and same-sex marriage.

Unfortunately, those sections of the document—its strongest—are not what have commanded public attention. The news coverage has focused on a single question. Although it is unfortunate that a complex message would be reduced to one issue, the single-minded coverage has not been entirely the fault of the mass media. Francis has himself to blame.

First, *Amoris Laetitia* is much too long. By publishing such a prolix document, the Holy Father increased the power of the intermediaries who, boiling it down for their readers, focus on that single issue.

Second, Francis himself encouraged the discussion of Communion for divorced-and-remarried Catholics, a discussion that was certain to become inflamed. To this day we do not know exactly what the Kasper proposal entails. The German cardinal proposed a "penitential path" by which divorced-and-remarried Catholics might be guided back to full communion, but he did not specify what that path would be. Nor do we know, even after the release of *Amoris Laetitia*, exactly what the pope has in mind for these couples, aside from a flexible and sympathetic pastoral approach.

The pope writes that in providing spiritual care for couples in irregular unions, pastors should adapt the general principles of Church teaching to particular circumstances: "It is a matter of reaching out to everyone, of needing to help each person find his or her proper way of participating in the ecclesial community and thus to experience being touched by an 'unmerited, unconditional and gratuitous' mercy" (297). Thus far his advice is unassailable. But in what cases would the pastor be justified in telling a couple that they should not feel bound by the laws of the Church—laws that reflect not mere arbitrary rules but divine commands? What sort of concrete circumstances would justify a break from the teaching—enunciated by Jesus Christ—that someone who leaves one spouse to live with another is engaged in an adulterous union?

There are, certainly, some circumstances in which the Church condones a second marital union. If a first marriage is annulled, the parties are free to remarry; and Francis has already streamlined the procedures for annulments, making it less likely that anyone who ought to receive an annulment will be denied. It is also possible, as St. John Paul II taught in *Familiaris Consortio*, for a divorced and remarried couple to be admitted to Communion if they agree to live as brother and sister. It is revealing that in the text of his lengthy apostolic exhortation, Francis never mentions the possibility of a couple's demonstrating their commitment to the Faith by abstaining from sexual relations. (The possibility is mentioned in a footnote, but the reader is left with the distinct impression that such discipline is to be discouraged.) Is that particular "penitential path," the one traditionally offered to Catholic couples in irregular unions, no longer worth discussing?

It is no secret that in some parts of the Catholic world, priests and pastors have already begun quietly to encourage divorced-and-remarried couples to receive Communion. In some places, particularly in the German-speaking world, lax pastoral practices are becoming the norm. Insofar as *Amoris Laetitia* encourages this practice, the vagueness of the pope's guidance undercuts the universality of Catholic teaching and discipline. After the publication of the apostolic exhortation, the German bishops quickly announced that they were ready to offer Communion to divorced-and-remarried couples, while the bishops of neighboring Poland were adamant that they would not. Robert Royal remarked:

> On one side of a border between two countries, Communion for the divorced and remarried would now become a sign of a new outpouring of God's mercy and forgiveness. On the other side, giving Communion to someone in "irregular" circumstances remains infidelity to Christ's words and, potentially, a sacrilege. In concrete terms, around the globe, what looms ahead is chaos and conflict, not Catholicity.

Francis downplays the importance of such conflicts in his apostolic exhortation—"not all discussions of doctrinal, moral, or pastoral issues need to be settled by interventions of the magisterium." True enough. But when the Magisterium *does* intervene, it is vitally important that that intervention be clear. The pope is a pastor, to be sure. But he is also a teacher—particularly when he is issuing an apostolic exhortation— and a teacher should be clear on matters of principle.

When, during another in-flight press conference, Francis was pressed about the meaning of footnote 351, surely the most contentious footnote in the recent history of the Church, he replied that he did not recall it. That answer strained credulity. Was the pope asking us to believe that he was unaware of the controversy? That he had forgotten the only words in his apostolic exhortation that directly addressed the most hotly contested question of the past two years? Had the fateful footnote been slipped in by an aide when Francis was not paying attention? Or was the pontiff struggling to preserve what American politicians call "plausible deniability," leaving it to others to draw out the implications of his work? Any one of those possibilities would reflect poorly on the pope.

That Francis was unaware of the contentious footnote is the least plausible explanation of his unwillingness to discuss it. His resort to such a transparent evasion suggested that he was not prepared to defend the argument that he had advanced in his own document. Had he expected the footnote to pass unnoticed? Or had he hoped that he could avoid any comment on the controversy and let others apply their own interpretations to his ambiguous teaching?

Unofficial Interpretations, Contradictory Readings

Father Antonio Spadaro, one of the pope's closest associates, issued his own pronouncement on the meaning of *Amoris Laetitia* in April 2016 in *La Civiltà Cattolica*. The pope, he declared, had

removed restrictions on the access of divorced-and-remarried Catholics to the Sacraments. That interpretation, which directly contradicts the assertion that the pope had made no major changes, was
notable because of its source. *La Civiltà Cattolica* is regarded as
semi-authoritative because its contents are approved in advance by
the Holy See's Secretariat of State. Spadaro, moreover, works closely
with Francis as adviser and translator and reportedly helped to draft
the apostolic exhortation.

The Vatican newspaper, *L'Osservatore Romano*, also weighed in,
giving front-page placement to an essay by Rocco Buttiglione—a widely
respected Italian philosopher, politician, and adviser to St. John Paul
II—in support of the argument that Catholics who are divorced and
remarried might, under some circumstances, receive Communion.
Reasoning that the Catholic Church has always recognized the possibility that individual circumstances determine whether or not someone is in a state of sin, Buttiglione writes:

> The path that the Pope proposes to divorced and remarried
> is exactly the same that the Church proposes to all sinners:
> Go to confession, and your confessor, after evaluating all the
> circumstances, will decide whether to absolve you and
> admit you to the Eucharist or not.

Buttiglione posits a case in which, he says, a confessor might justifiably instruct a divorced and remarried person to receive the Eucharist. A woman, abandoned by her first husband, marries again, has
children, and then returns to the practice of the Faith. She herself
might be willing to abstain from sexual activity, but her new partner,
insisting on his marital rights, threatens to leave her—and their children—if she does not share his bed. The risk of breaking up the family,
which would seriously harm the children, is unacceptable, Buttiglione
argues, so the woman is not at fault for consenting to intercourse and

should be admitted to Communion. But there are three glaring problems with this scenario.

First, Christ himself taught that if a woman "divorces her husband and marries another, she commits adultery" (Mark 10:12). If the confessor admitted this woman to Communion, wouldn't he be saying that adultery can be justified in some circumstances? It is a fundamental moral principle that certain acts (adultery among them), judged by the objective norms of morality, are intrinsically evil. Such acts are never justified by one's intention or circumstances. As the *Catechism of the Catholic Church* (paragraph 1756) explains,

> It is therefore an error to judge the morality of human acts by considering only the intention that inspires them or the circumstances (environment, social pressure, duress or emergency, etc.) which supply their context. There are acts which, in and of themselves, independently of circumstances and intentions, are always gravely illicit by reason of their object; such as blasphemy and perjury, murder and adultery. One may not do evil so that good may result from it.

Second, if a confessor counseled this woman to submit to her new partner's demands—sleep with me or your children go hungry—would he be enabling an abusive relationship? What other demands, physical or emotional, might the second husband be making of which the confessor was unaware? Imagine the storm of (justified) criticism if it were known, or even suspected, that priests were instructing meek women to endure spousal abuse.

Third, Buttiglione assumes that a couple should remain together, even in an illicit marriage, for the sake of their children. But that assumption contradicts the understanding of marriage set forth by a previous pontiff. In his 1930 encyclical *Casti Connubii*, Pius XI, quoting St. Augustine, wrote that the marriage bond is so sacred that "a husband or wife, if separated, should not be joined to another even for the sake of offspring."

Buttiglione at least attempted to come up with a case in which the Kasper proposal could be reconciled with Church teaching. One frustrating aspect of the debate was the refusal of Kasper and his many supporters to explain under what circumstances divorced and remarried Catholics might be allowed to receive Communion or to elaborate on the process by which couples might reach that decision. Acknowledging that the decision should not be taken lightly, they stipulated that remarried couples should go through a "process of reconciliation" before approaching the Eucharist. But what was that process, and who should determine whether, at last, they were ready for Communion? Those simple and obvious questions were never answered.

Many of Kasper's supporters hinted at something like Buttiglione's scenario, discussing circumstances in which it might be a hardship for a remarried couple to abstain from sexual activity. Yes, it could certainly be a hardship. But sometimes moral decisions require hard choices. Many married couples are forced to abstain from intercourse for other reasons—a medical condition, perhaps, or a physical separation. It is a hardship but not an impossibility.

The absence of any details about the proposed "process of reconciliation" opens a wide door for abuse of any new policy. Advocates of the Kasper proposal invariably say that the Church's age-old rules should be applied in *most* cases, that the new dispensation would be offered only to a few. But the proposal's reliance on the "internal forum" leaves the final determination in each case up to the individual confessor, practically inviting couples to "forum shop" for a priest with an expansive view of the new policy's applicability. Priests who are inclined to be more rigorous will soon realize that they are fighting a losing battle as disappointed penitents drive across town to a more compliant confessor. A policy that was introduced as an exception could quickly become the new norm.

The prospect of introducing teachings or disciplines that could undermine the sanctity of marriage is unacceptable to Catholic bishops in some parts of the world. The South African cardinal Wilfrid Napier, employing a quintessentially First-World means of communication to question the logic of *Amoris Laetitia*, tweeted, "If Westerners in irregular situations can receive Communion, are we to tell our polygamists & other 'misfits' that they too are allowed?"

A Silence that Undermined the Law

Other parts of the world, however, have welcomed a more open-ended reading of *Amoris Laetitia*. The bishops in the pope's hometown of Buenos Aires, preparing instructions for their pastors on the implementation of *Amoris Laetitia*, embraced the Kasper proposal, encouraging the "pastoral accompaniment" of couples in irregular unions, with the understanding that even if they persist in such relationships "a path of discernment" that could lead them to the Eucharist "is possible."

In a private letter sent to these bishops in early September 2016, Francis congratulated his countrymen on their interpretation of his apostolic exhortation, writing that it "fully captures the meaning" of his work. "There are no other interpretations," he added.

When this letter was leaked to the press (and confirmed as authentic by the Holy See several days later), the world's Catholics were subjected to an absurd spectacle. After more than two years of highly contentious debate—first about the Kasper proposal and then about the meaning of a single footnote in the longest papal document in history—without any clear guidance from the pope, the first seemingly authoritative interpretation finally emerged, not in a formal public statement but in a private letter in which the pontiff was commenting on *someone else's* interpretation.

Wouldn't it have been more sensible to resolve such a question with a formal statement from the Vatican press office? Yet once again,

Francis deliberately avoided putting any such statement on the record. Just a few months earlier, responding to the same old question from reporters during an in-flight interview, he had declined to give a direct answer. Andrea Tornielli of *La Stampa* recalled:

> He was asked whether there were any real new possibilities for access to the sacraments that did not exist prior to the publication of the *"Amoris Laetitia"* encyclical [*sic*]. "I could say 'yes' and leave it at that," Francis had replied. "But that would be too brief a response. I recommend that all of you read the presentation made by Cardinal Schönborn, a great theologian."

If Francis were to declare clearly and formally that divorced and remarried Catholics might receive Communion, he would have to ignore the strong resistance that he encountered in the Synod, undermining his claim to be speaking on behalf of the world's bishops. He would also have to contradict the teaching of John Paul II, who stated in *Familiaris Consortio* that divorced-and-remarried Catholics must live as brothers and sisters if they wish to approach the Eucharist. If they were otherwise admitted to Communion, John Paul wrote, "the faithful would be led into error and confusion regarding the Church's teaching about the indissolubility of marriage" (84). The logic of that magisterial statement is compelling. And if Francis reversed the policy set by John Paul II, it would seem clear that a future pontiff could reverse the policy set by Francis, and *no* papal statement on this question could be regarded as conclusive.

Despite his studied ambiguity, Francis has unquestionably opened a door for the divorced and remarried to receive Communion. As a practical matter, virtually every divorced and remarried Catholic can argue that *his* case falls into that special category—whatever it is—of those allowed to receive the Eucharist. If his pastor disagrees, he will probably move on to another parish, until he finds a pastor who accepts his argument.

Was that the pope's intent: to leave every parish priest free to make his own interpretations of Church teaching? Having spoken frequently about decentralization of Church authority, did the pope really mean to go that far? He has playfully encouraged young Catholics to "make a mess"; was he trying to set an example by deconstructing the teaching office?

The Code of Canon Law puts priests under a solemn obligation to avoid scandal by withholding the Eucharist from those who persist in manifest grave sin (canon 915). An adulterous relationship is a manifest grave sin. The Argentine bishops appear to say—with papal approval—that in some circumstances priests should administer Communion to people who are living in objectively adulterous relationships. Has canon 915 been amended or abrogated, then? The pope is the supreme legislator of the Church, with the unquestioned power to modify canon law. But he has not done so. In fact, he has deliberately avoided the exercise of his authority, giving the impression that formal Church teachings and laws do not really matter and can safely be ignored.

The Four Cardinals and the Dubia

The confusion generated by *Amoris Laetitia* and the resulting threat to Catholic unity prompted four cardinals—Walter Brandmül-ler, Raymond Burke, Carlo Caffarra, and Joachim Meisner[2]—to write to the pontiff in September 2016 pleading for clarification, observing that "divergent" and even "conflicting" interpretations of Chapter 8 of

---

2 The German Brandmüller, a Church historian, was appointed a cardinal by Benedict XVI at the age of eighty-one and thus was never eligible to vote in a papal conclave. Burke, an American, was the prefect of the Apostolic Signatura until Francis removed him in 2014 in a striking gesture of disfavor. Caffarra, the founder of the Pontifical John Paul II Institute for Studies on Marriage and Family, retired as archbishop of Bologna in 2015 and died in September 2017. Meisner, who was close to John Paul II and Benedict XVI, retired as archbishop of Cologne in 2014 and died in July 2017.

the exhortation had provoked "uncertainty, confusion and disorienta-tion among many of the faithful" regarding the Church's teaching on marriage. "[C]ompelled in conscience by [their] pastoral responsibil-ity," the cardinals submitted to the pope "as supreme teacher of the faith" the following five questions—*dubia*—about the exhortation, asking him "to resolve the uncertainties and bring clarity":

1. Is it now "possible to grant absolution in the sacrament of penance and thus to admit to holy Communion a person who, while bound by a valid marital bond, lives together with a different person *more uxorio* [as man and wife]"? And "[c]an the expression 'in certain cases' found in Note 351... be applied to divorced persons who are in a new union and who continue to live *more uxorio*?"

2. "[D]oes one still need to regard as valid the teaching of St. John Paul II's encyclical *Veritatis splendor*, 79, based on sacred Scripture and on the Tradition of the Church, on the existence of absolute moral norms that prohibit intrinsically evil acts and that are binding without excep-tions?"

3. "[I]s it still possible to affirm that a person who habitually lives in contradiction to a commandment of God's law, as for instance the one that prohibits adultery (Matthew 19:3–9), finds him or herself in an objective situation of grave habitual sin...?"

4. "[D]oes one still need to regard as valid the teaching of St. John Paul II's encyclical *Veritatis splendor*, 81,... according to which 'circumstances or intentions can never transform an act intrinsically evil by virtue of its object into an act "subjectively" good or defensible as a choice'"?

5. "[D]oes one still need to regard as valid the teaching of St. John Paul II's encyclical *Veritatis Splendor*, 56,... that

conscience can never be authorized to legitimate excep-
tions to absolute moral norms that prohibit intrinsically
evil acts by virtue of their object?"

After waiting patiently for several weeks without a reply, the four
cardinals presented their questions—each of which can be answered
simply "yes" or "no"—to the universal Church for discussion, explaining that they interpreted the pontiff's silence as "an invitation to continue the reflection, and the discussion, calmly and with respect."

The staunchest defenders of Francis professed shock at the public
appeal, calling it an act of disrespect for the supreme pontiff, but Cardinal George Pell rejected that criticism. The four cardinals, he
observed, were merely raising questions, and significant questions at
that, not fomenting dissent: "How can you disagree with a question?"

Msgr. Pio Vito Pinto, the dean of the Roman Rota, took a very different line. Outraged by the cardinals' letter, he said that the pope could
remove the four prelates from the College of Cardinals as punishment
for their effrontery. Cardinals Burke, Brandmüller, Caffarra, and Meisner could be charged with causing "grave scandal," Pinto declared, for
their questions about the interpretation of an apostolic exhortation that
reflects the work of the Synod of Bishops—begging the question whether
the apostolic exhortation *does* reflect the work of the Synod of Bishops.
"The action of the Holy Spirit cannot be doubted," Pinto insisted.

Still the pope was silent, offering no public response to the *dubia*.
In November 2016 he convened a consistory to confer red hats on
seventeen new cardinals. Before his previous two consistories, Francis
had held days of discussion with the members of the College. This time,
however, he did not bring the cardinals together apart from the formal
ceremony, prompting the Vatican journalist Marco Tosatti to speculate
that he feared some "cardinals, eager for a decisive word from the
Pope," might seize the occasion to re-submit the *dubia*.

Cardinal Gerhard Müller, the prefect of the Congregation for the
Doctrine of the Faith, said that his office could respond to the *dubia* if

the pope authorized him to do so. Since his congregation issues judgments "with the authority of the Pope," he noted, it would be inappropriate to intervene without the pope's approval.

Reports of a battle inside the Vatican over the interpretation of *Amoris Laetitia* were overblown, said Cardinal Müller, and reflected the tendency of reporters to interpret Church affairs in terms of power politics. At the same time, he said, it is important for the faithful to "remain objective and not be drawn into polarization." To the most controversial question about *Amoris Laetitia*—whether divorced and remarried Catholics can be admitted to Communion—Müller declined to give a direct answer.

While Müller expressed confidence that *Amoris Laetitia* is fully compatible with previous Church teachings, the Italian cardinal who had signed the *dubia* disagreed. Carlo Caffarra remarked that "only a blind man could deny that there's great confusion, uncertainty, and insecurity in the Church." In an interview with the Italian daily *Il Foglio*, Caffarra said that the confusion involves "extremely serious questions for the life of the Church and the eternal salvation of the faithful."

"In recent months," Caffarra said, "on some very fundamental questions regarding the sacraments, such as marriage, confession and the Eucharist, and the Christian life in general," diocesan bishops have issued contradictory interpretations of the pope's words and announced radically different policies. "There is only one way to get to the bottom" of the confusion, he reasoned: "to ask the author of the text." He decried as "false and calumnious" the charge that the *dubia* have caused divisions within the Church. "The division that already exists in the Church is the cause, not the effect," of the plea for papal clarification, he said.

But the desire for clarity is itself the problem, suggested Archbishop Mark Coleridge of Brisbane, Australia. In an interview published in *America*, he warned that the prelates seeking clarification were pursuing a "false clarity that comes because you don't address reality." In the Synod sessions, Coleridge "heard voices that sounded very clear and certain but only because they never grappled with the real question or never dealt with the real facts." While some people prefer to see things in black and white, he said, pastors are "very often dealing in a world of grays and you have to accompany people, listen to them before you speak to them, give them time and give them space, and then speak your word perhaps." The archbishop did not explain how moral clarity might be incompatible with "real facts," but it is often incompatible with what we *desire*.

Coleridge conceded that many Catholics have been "unnerved" by the papal document, as his countryman Cardinal Pell had suggested. "Some people expect from the Pope clarity and certainty on every question and every issue," said Coleridge, "but a pastor can't provide that necessarily."

The Ambiguity Is Intentional

As weeks turned into months and the *dubia* remained unanswered, it became increasingly clear that the pope's silence was strategic. The confusion in *Amoris Laetitia* is not a bug; it is a feature.

The defenders of the apostolic exhortation insisted that its notorious eighth chapter was clear enough and that the four cardinals who raised questions about its meaning were merely being argumentative. But if that were the case, the pontiff could have avoided this public embarrassment by answering the cardinals' questions. He has chosen not to do so.

There are only three possible ways to interpret the pope's silence. Either he was being remarkably rude to his closest counselors, flatly refusing to answer their honest questions, or he did not want to give a straight answer. Or both.

The one possibility that can be quickly excluded from discussion is that the pope believed the meaning of *Amoris Laetitia* was already clear to the faithful. It was not. After two years of intense debate on the most controversial question involved, intelligent and informed Catholics were still unsure as to what exactly Francis had taught.

If the papal teaching were clear, how could it mean one thing in Poland and another in Germany, one thing in Philadelphia and Portland and another in Chicago and San Diego? If some bishops were interpreting the papal document incorrectly, why had they not been corrected?

As the four conscientious cardinals continued to press the pope for clarification, some Catholic reporters tried to determine how long it ordinarily takes for a pope to respond to *dubia* of this sort. There is no good answer to that question, because there is no precedent for this query. Ordinarily, papal documents are clear. If any confusion arises from papal statements, a clarification usually follows quickly— long before any formal *dubium* can be raised—because the very *point* of papal teaching is to provide clarity. Usually. But this was a different case.

John Allen, writing at *Crux*, offered a plausible reading of the pope's intentions: "Maybe this is his version of Catholic R&D, letting things play out for a while on the ground before he says anything irreversible." In other words, maybe the pope is deliberately making room for pastoral experimentation, to see what works. Archbishop Coleridge seemed comfortable with that approach. "Pastoral care moves within ambiguity," he wrote on his Twitter account, adding a dig at the four cardinals: "We now need a pastoral patience not the quick-fix anxiety voiced here."

If Allen and Coleridge believed that the pope was encouraging experimentation by leaving matters unsettled, another observer—one much closer to the pope—insisted that the meaning of *Amoris Laetitia* had been settled. Father Antonio Spadaro reacted to the four cardinals' public letter with a furious tweet-storm. "The Pope has 'clarified,'" the Jesuit began. "Those who don't like what they hear pretend not to hear it!" He included a link to the pope's letter to the Argentine bishops, as if a leaked private letter bore any authority. And, of course, the Argentine bishops' policy did not address the *dubia*. Taunting the four cardinals, Spadaro later tweeted, "*Amoris Laetitia* is an act of the

Magisterium (card. Schönborn) so don't keep asking the same question until you get the answer *you* want...."

Credited with a major role in drafting *Amoris Laetitia*, Spadaro may have revealed more on Twitter than just a splenetic temper. If he wanted the cardinals to stop asking difficult questions, it is not unreasonable to suspect that the pope himself wants to bury those questions. And the pope's continued silence reinforces that suspicion.

Defending the Pope, Avoiding the Issue

"All I know is that the doubts that are there, that are expressed, aren't my doubts, and I think they're not the doubts of the universal Church," Cardinal Blase Cupich reassured Edward Pentin of the *National Catholic Register* in answer to a question about the *dubia*. Unperturbed by any ambiguities, the archbishop of Chicago continued:

> The document that they're having doubts about is the fruit of two synods, and the fruit of propositions that were voted on by two-thirds of the bishops who were there. It is a post-synodal apostolic exhortation and so it stands on the same level as all the other post-synodal apostolic exhortations as a magisterial document. I think that if you begin to question the legitimacy of what is being said in such a document, do you then throw into question then [sic] all of the other documents that have been issued before by the other popes?

Actually, as Pentin observed, the propositions in question were *not* approved by the Synod of Bishops. But that was almost beside the point, because the four cardinals were not expressing doubts about what the Synod said. They were not even directly questioning the pope's summary of the Synod's deliberations. They were questioning *some persons' interpretation* of the pope's document summarizing the Synod.

To raise questions about *Amoris Laetitia*, Cupich suggests, even questions about how it should be understood, is to call into question all previous papal statements. A more nuanced approach to the Magisterium, however, may be necessary. In raising their *dubia*, the four cardinals observed that some interpretations of *Amoris Laetitia* appear to conflict directly with *Veritatis Splendor*, the magisterial work of St. John Paul II. If one papal pronouncement appears to contradict another, the conflict cannot be resolved by saying that all good Catholics should accept the authority of papal documents.

Another of Francis's new American cardinals, Joseph Tobin of Newark, also tried to sidestep the issues raised in the *dubia*. "[W]hat would really be helpful is that rather than each individual bishop or cardinal demanding that the pope pronounce on every concrete application of the magisterium, that we as bishops suck it up and do what we're supposed to do." That might make sense if the bishops knew what they were supposed to do. But the *dubia* address the point that many bishops do not know what they are supposed to do. For that matter, some bishops who are quite confident that they know what to do are at odds with others equally confident that *they* know what to do.

The confusion surrounding the papal document is evident. There are two ways to address it. One is by answering the cardinals' questions. The other is by imitating Rex Mottram, a comical dunce in Evelyn Waugh's *Brideshead Revisited*. The Jesuit priest who has undertaken the task of instructing the insincere Mottram in the Catholic Faith reports with exasperation,

> Yesterday I asked him whether Our Lord had more than one nature. He said: "Just as many as you say, Father." Then again I asked him: "Supposing the Pope looked up and saw a cloud and said "It's going to rain," would that be bound to happen?" "Oh, yes, Father." "But supposing it didn't?" He thought a moment and said, "I suppose it would be sort of raining spiritually, only we were too sinful to see it."

Cardinal Marx of Munich opted for the Mottram approach, telling the *National Catholic Register* that the German bishops' conference had no difficulty in reaching agreement on the proper interpretation of *Amoris Laetitia*. They issued guidelines, reflecting "a clear position," for the admission of divorced and remarried Catholics to Communion in some cases.

Father Spadaro of *La Civiltà Cattolica* took the same line, insisting that the four cardinals' questions had already been answered. Conceding that the *dubia* involved "interesting" questions, he said that they "were already raised during the Synod," where "all of the necessary responses were given, and more than once." In another obvious slap at the cardinals who had raised the *dubia*, the combative Spadaro said that "a doubtful conscience can easily find all of the answers it seeks, if it seeks them with sincerity." Lest anyone miss his point, he went on to say that the discussion of *Amoris Laetitia* should exclude "those who use criticism for other purposes or ask questions in order to create difficulty or division."

Spadaro outdid himself in January 2017 when he posted a cryptic comment on his Twitter account ridiculing those who sought certainty about the papal teaching:

Theology is no #Mathematics. 2 + 2 in #Theology can make
5. Because it has to do with #God and real #life of #people…

Was Spadaro suggesting that when we speak about "real life," the rules of logic don't apply? If someone tells you, "You can talk all you want about the law of gravity, but in real life…," you won't know what is coming next, but you know it will be nonsense. The law of gravity is a law of real life, which applies to real people.

So how is it possible that "2 + 2 in #Theology can make 5"? Spadaro tells us that theology "has to do with God." Does he mean, then, that God might violate the laws of logic? If so, he has plunged into the error that Benedict XVI critiqued in his famous Regensburg address: the notion that faith cannot be subject to rational analysis. Benedict saw this disparagement of reason as a weakness of Islamic thought. He probably never anticipated that the problem would crop up in the editorial offices of *La Civiltà Cattolica*.

If Spadaro can suspend the ordinary rule of logic with vague references to "real life" and "people," then he can sew up the debate on *Amoris Laetitia* very neatly. Every case is different—so the argument goes—and therefore no general laws can apply. By that logic, since every stone you toss up in the air is different, you can never be sure that the stone will come down.

Another possible interpretation of Spadaro's curious tweet is no more reassuring. He may have been suggesting that you and I and millions of other ordinary Catholics cannot be expected to follow the intricate logic of theologians—just as we are flummoxed by the abstruse calculations of quantum mechanics. We should therefore leave this important business to the professionals. In other words, we should accept what we're told. We are not expected to understand; we are only expected to fall in line. Spadaro's approach to faith is not based on reason. It may, however, be based on power.

As far as I can discern it, Spadaro's argument against the *dubia* runs like this: We cannot lay down black-and-white rules for marriage and divorce cases because the circumstances of every case are different. That's perfectly true. But isn't the purpose of marriage tribunals to examine the circumstances of individual cases and to apply the general rules to those circumstances? If there are no general rules to be applied, then the tribunals (or the pastors, in the *Amoris Laetitia* dispensation) will be operating in a vacuum.

If we apply the same logic to another, less controversial field, we immediately recognize the absurdity:

> Experienced tennis umpires know that there are many marginal calls. Whether the ball is called "in" or "out" is influenced by a number of different factors: the angle of the shot,

the position of the line judge, the condition of the court. No two shots are alike. Therefore, only abstract theorists of the game would want the lines drawn on the tennis court before the match.

The Same "Talking Points"

It has become obvious that close associates of Francis, the defenders of *Amoris Laetitia,* and the critics of the four cardinals are all reading from the same script. The similarity in the arguments presented—even the phrases used—points to someone somewhere at the Vatican who has put together "talking points" for those who want to debunk the *dubia.* It is possible to discern at least seven:

1. *Don't talk about the* dubia. The goal is not to answer the *dubia* but to sweep them off the table. The pope's allies do not mention the questions that the four cardinals have actually asked, for they might sound too reasonable. They try to give the impression that the cardinals are asking trick questions or probing into arcana. Above all, they do not admit that the *dubia* would allow for a simple yes-or-no answer.
2. *Insist that* Amoris Laetitia *is perfectly clear.* The papal defenders cite each other's remarks about the document's alleged clarity but do not acknowledge that authoritative commentators have said the opposite. In the alternative, they say that the document is *intentionally* unclear, because ambiguity is necessary to preserve the pastor's room for discretion in handling difficult cases.
3. *Poke fun at the traditional Church teaching and at the old-fashioned pastors who uphold it.* In speaking to the secular media, the allies play upon popular prejudices and sympathies.

4. *Say that the* dubia *reflect a simplistic approach.* The document is perfectly clear, its advocates say, but the recommendations call for a more nuanced understanding. The archbishop of Dublin, Diarmuid Martin, has lamented that some people "are unsettled by the ability of the Pope to place himself in the midst of the uncertainties of people's lives."

5. *Come down hard on papal authority.* Never mind that the four cardinals are only asking questions. Never mind that *Amoris Laetitia* seems directly to contradict previous papal teachings, so *some* papal teaching must be questioned. Never mind that Francis himself has called for free debate and encouraged people to "make a mess." Hammer away on papal authority. Suggest that those who question the papal document are undermining the principle of infallibility (when in fact the questions are intended to preserve the constancy of Church teaching).

6. *Don't be afraid to impugn the integrity of people who disagree.* The British journalist Austen Ivereigh writes of an "anti-Francis revolt" that had taken on "a newly vicious tone"—before proceeding with his own vicious attack on critics of *Amoris Laetitia*.

7. *Paint a rosy picture of relationships between Catholics and their pastors.* The Kasper proposal presumes that a divorced and remarried Catholic has engaged in a deep and lengthy examination of conscience, aided by a discerning pastor. Such a penitent-confessor relationship is taken as the norm, although in reality it is surely the rare exception.

These "talking points" are not consistent with each other. It makes no sense, for instance, to insist on papal authority, piously invoking the principle "Rome has spoken," in defense of Rome's *failure* to speak.

But this rhetorical strategy is intended not to *win* the argument but to *squelch* it—to silence the pope's critics or, failing that, to persuade others to ignore them.

It should come as no surprise that the self-contradiction on which the defense of *Amoris Laetitia* is based—the apostolic exhortation changes no doctrine, yet some divorced and remarried Catholics may now receive Communion—leads to occasional tactical confusion. In February 2017, the Vatican press published a booklet by Cardinal Francesco Coccopalmerio, *The Eighth Chapter of the Post-Synodal Apostolic Exhortation Amoris Laetitia*, whose forty pages are devoted to that very self-contradiction. Coccopalmerio declares that *Amoris Laetitia* expresses "with absolute clarity all the elements of the doctrine on marriage in full consistency and fidelity to the traditional teachings of the Church." He goes on to maintain that insisting on sexual continence in a second union can threaten that union and therefore the welfare of children. In such a case, a person may "be in a concrete situation which does not allow him or her to act differently and decide otherwise without further sin." Catholics in such a union may receive the Eucharist if they "wish to change this situation, but cannot realize their desire." This interpretation of *Amoris Laetitia* conflicts directly with what Cardinal Müller said when he was the head of the Congregation for the Doctrine of the Faith.

Coccopalmerio's position as the Vatican's top canon lawyer and his booklet's publication by the Vatican press gave the impression that the work was a semi-official response to questions about the proper interpretation of *Amoris Laetitia*—that is, an answer to the *dubia*. That impression was strengthened by the announcement of a press conference at the Vatican on February 14 to introduce the booklet. Then to everyone's surprise, Coccopalmerio failed to appear at that press conference, leaving a theology professor and an Italian journalist to introduce his work. And though the booklet had been touted in advance as the final answer to the much-discussed questions about *Amoris*

Laetitia, the director of the Vatican press—Coccopalmerio's pub-lisher—conceded that "the debate is still open."

The excuse later offered for Coccopalmerio's absence, a scheduling conflict, was implausible—as if the publisher hadn't thought of con-firming the author's availability before scheduling the press conference. If the cardinal's booklet and the publicity surrounding its release were designed to quiet rumors of discord and intrigue within the Vatican over *Amoris Laetitia*, they had the opposite effect.

The rumors of discord and intrigue had grown when Edward Pentin reported in the *National Catholic Register* that the Congregation for the Doctrine of the Faith had recommended a number of changes to *Amoris Laetitia* at the draft stage, but "not one of the corrections was accepted." Pentin's report appeared to corroborate an earlier story by Jean-Marie Guénois in *Le Figaro* that the Vatican's doctrinal office had submitted twenty pages of suggested modifications before the apostolic exhortation was made public—apparently all to no avail.

Another sort of intrigue was exposed by Michael Pakaluk, a profes-sor of ethics at the Catholic University of America, who discovered that one passage of *Amoris Laetitia* was copied from an essay written more than twenty years earlier by a close associate of the pontiff. Writing in *Crux*, Pakaluk shows that an important sentence in the controversial Chapter 8 and other passages were drawn almost verbatim from an article published in 1995 by Archbishop Victor Manuel Fernández, now the rector of the Catholic University of Argentina and an adviser to the pope. Fernández is believed to have been the ghostwriter of the encycli-cal *Laudato Si'* and to have had a major role in drafting *Amoris Laetitia*.

The unacknowledged use of material from an earlier essay raises new questions about the papal document. Ordinarily, Pakaluk writes, "an explicit quotation [in a papal document] of a theological journal article would be received as having its own distinctive force and weight. To say about it, then, in an unqualified way, 'it is the magisterium,' would be a kind of spiritual bullying."

Moreover, Pakaluk points out that the sentence appropriated in Chapter 8, concerning St. Thomas Aquinas's teaching about the consequences of difficulties in exercising particular virtues, distorts St. Thomas and was put to theologically troubling use in Fernández's 1995 article. Did Fernández exploit his position as papal adviser (and perhaps ghostwriter) to give his own controversial ideas the stamp of papal approval? And did he needlessly embarrass the pontiff by appropriating his own words without attribution? As Pakaluk observes, "In secular contexts, a ghostwriter who exposed the author he was serving to charges of plagiarism would be dismissed as reckless." But with *Amoris Laetitia*, that sort of confusion has been the norm.

The Limits of Papal Authority

Within the Catholic Church, the authority of the Roman pontiff is considerable. But even papal authority—and especially papal infallibility—has its limits. The pope speaks with authority when he sets forth the Deposit of Faith, explaining, in union with the College of Bishops, what the Church has always and everywhere believed. In the case of *Amoris Laetitia*, the two meetings of the Synod of Bishops made it clear that the pope was not in union with all the world's bishops on the Kasper proposal. But leaving that disagreement aside, anyone who understands the nature of the Petrine power should recognize that, even when he speaks on questions of faith and morals, there are some things the pope cannot say. For instance:

The Pope cannot say that 2+2=5. Nor can he repeal the laws of logic. So if the pope makes two contradictory statements, they cannot both be right. And since every pontiff enjoys the same teaching authority, if one pope contradicts another pope, something is wrong. Thus if *Amoris Laetitia* contradicts *Veritatis Splendor* and *Casti Connubii*— earlier papal encyclicals, which carry a higher level of teaching authority—the faithful cannot be obliged to swallow the contradiction.

The pope cannot tell Catholics what they think. He can, within certain limitations, tell them what they *should* think. But he cannot, simply by the force of his authority, change minds. The pope's supporters insist that *Amoris Laetitia* is perfectly clear. "The Pope leaves no room for doubt about the teaching of the Church," asserts Father Spadaro. Even if that statement came directly from the pope himself (which it did not, obviously), it could not be authoritative. If someone has doubts, then evidently there is room for doubt; not even the pope can gainsay that fact. Ideally the pope and those speaking for him would help Catholics to resolve those doubts, rather than suggesting that doubt implies disloyalty.

The pope cannot teach authoritatively by dropping hints. On the most controversial issue discussed at the two meetings of the Synod of Bishops devoted to marriage and the family, *Amoris Laetitia* is vague, allowing for radically different interpretations. Father Spadaro and Cardinal Schönborn and the Argentine bishops can all make a compelling argument that they know what Francis had in mind—especially because the Holy Father himself has endorsed their interpretations. But what the pope *had in mind* does not carry the same weight as what the pope *actually wrote*. And that is especially true when there is such abundant evidence that he *deliberately* left the question unresolved:

- The pope avoided addressing the question directly in his apostolic exhortation, left the clearest evidence of his intention in an obscure footnote, and then later told reporters that he didn't remember that footnote.
- Francis endorsed the Argentine bishops' interpretation in a private letter and Schönborn's interpretation in an interview with the press. Obviously neither was a formal statement of the Magisterium.
- He declined to answer the *dubia* submitted by four cardinals.

- According to Archbishop Bruno Forte—a noted theologian, whose sympathies are generally with Pope Francis and who played a key role in drafting the first report of the Synod on the Family—the pontiff told him during the Synod session, "If we speak explicitly about communion for the divorced and remarried, you do not know what a terrible mess we will make. So we won't speak plainly, do it in a way that the premises are there, then I will draw out the conclusions."

By now it should be clear that in *Amoris Laetitia*, Francis carefully avoids making the sort of authoritative statement that would command the assent of the faithful. Catholics cannot be expected—much less commanded—to accept a new "teaching" that the pope has chosen, for his own reasons, *not* to make.

A Test of Orthodoxy—or Something Else?

In July 2017, Cardinal Christoph Schönborn—routinely identified as the "authoritative interpreter" of *Amoris Laetitia*—addressed an Irish audience about the document. Earlier, he had said that the notorious footnote 351, indicating that pastoral outreach to divorced and remarried Catholics "can include the help of the sacraments," refers primarily to the Sacrament of Penance. Now the cardinal said that questions about the reception of Communion were a "trap," because the real emphasis should be on an examination of conscience. Pastors, he said, should help couples evaluate their individual circumstances with an eye to answering the critical question, "What is the possible good that a person or a couple can achieve in difficult circumstances?"

"If we consider the immense variety of situations it is understandable that neither the synod nor this exhortation could be expected to provide a new set of general rules, canonical in nature, and applicable to all cases," Schönborn reasoned. But prior to *Amoris Laetitia*, the clear teaching of the Church *had* provided a rule that applied to all cases: Catholics involved in a second marital union when their previous spouse was alive could not receive Communion unless they undertook to live as brother and sister. So even as he professed that Church teaching had not changed, he indicated that pastoral practice should change, indicating a willingness to compromise on that teaching.

Schönborn took a dim view of his fellow cardinals who were still pleading for a clarification. Conceding that cardinals have a right to speak with the pontiff about a contentious issue, he nevertheless criticized those who had made their request a matter of public record:

> That cardinals, who should be the closest collaborators of the pope, try to force him, to put pressure on him to give a public response to their publicized, personal letter to the pope—this is absolutely inconvenient behavior, I'm sorry to say. If they want to have an audience with the pope, they ask for an audience; but they do not publish that they asked for an audience.

Something was lost in translation here. When Schönborn said the public questioning of the pope was "inconvenient," he surely meant "inappropriate." For his part, the cardinal believes that the pope *has* made significant changes in Church teaching. Yet he also insists that *Amoris Laetitia* is fully in line with previous Church teaching. According to Austen Ivereigh's sympathetic account of the address in Ireland,

> Schönborn revealed that when he met the Pope shortly after the presentation of *Amoris*, Francis thanked him, and asked him if the document was orthodox.
> "I said, 'Holy Father, it is fully orthodox'," Schönborn told us he told the pope, adding that a few days later he

received from Francis a little note that said: "Thank you for that word. That gave me comfort."

Assuming its accuracy (which we have no reason to doubt), Schönborn's anecdote presents us with an astonishing picture: The successor to St. Peter—the man whose solemn duty it is to guard the Deposit of Faith—is asking another prelate whether his own teaching is orthodox. And he is comforted to hear an affirmative answer.

It is to be expected that Francis consults with Schönborn, one of his close advisers and a respected theologian. But he apparently sought assurance of his writing's orthodoxy *after* the document had been issued. Publishing the document first and soliciting opinions about its doctrinal soundness later bespeaks a dangerously insouciant approach to the integrity of the Faith.

Is it possible that Francis was not entirely sure about the orthodoxy of *Amoris Laetitia* even after he released it? At the very least, his taking "comfort" in Schönborn's reassurance indicates that the pope knew some influential prelates would find the document unsound.

But is there, perhaps, another way to look at the pope's request for Schönborn's opinion? Maybe Francis was not so much curious about the orthodoxy of his apostolic exhortation as he was interested in gauging the reliability of Cardinal Schönborn. The Austrian was respected by his colleagues as a serious theologian and known as a student and confidant of the retired Benedict XVI. If he could count on Schönborn's support in the campaign for acceptance of *Amoris Laetitia*, the pope would indeed be comforted. Schönborn would be an important ally, and the pope knew that he faced a major battle.

CHAPTER SEVEN

Allies and Enemies

B y 2016, as the debate on *Amoris Laetitia* intensified, clear lines of division had become visible within the Catholic Church. The pope's critics were more outspoken, and his defenders were more acerbic in response.

In October, *Vatican Insider* published a troubling article by the Italian journalists Giacomo Galeazzi and Andrea Tornielli under the inflammatory headline "Catholics Who Are Anti-Francis but Love Putin." "The attack against Francis is global," they warned breathlessly. Treating groups and individuals with very different ideas and priorities as if they formed a united front of opposition to the papacy, the authors depicted anyone who has questioned public statements by Francis not as a loyal critic but as an "enemy."

Galeazzi and Tornielli are respected reporters for *La Stampa* with solid sources, Tornielli in particular enjoying extensive access to insiders in Francis's Vatican. As they are not ordinarily prone to sensationalism, the charge that the pope's critics are more supportive of a Russian strongman than of the Vicar of Christ probably reflects what they had heard from their contacts inside the Vatican. If so, then some of the people surrounding Francis have come to believe that the pontiff is the target of a budding conspiracy. Having adopted a paranoid style, they see enemies wherever there is resistance to their agenda. Or still worse, they simply find it useful, for their own Machiavellian purposes, to broadcast the conspiracy theory.

Francis undoubtedly has his critics, as does any public figure, but the *Vatican Insider* article fails to distinguish among them. Such an analysis, ignoring the differences not only in their tone (some harsh and hostile, others cautious and respectful) but also in their prescriptions, collapses under its own weight. After suggesting the existence of a conspiracy, Galeazzi and Tornielli quote the sociologist Massimo Introvigne as saying that the effort against Francis "is not successful because it is not united." Indeed, it is not. Someone worried about the pastoral consequences of *Amoris Laetitia* is not likely to repudiate the Second Vatican Council's stand on religious freedom. Someone with reservations about open borders does not necessarily long for the return of Benedict XVI. The conspiracy is in the minds of Galeazzi and Tornielli—and perhaps their sources inside the Vatican.

The most curious entry in the list of the papal "enemies" identified by *Vatican Insider* might be the Chinese Catholics worried about the state of negotiations between the Vatican and Beijing. The negotiations were designed, from the Vatican's perspective, to end the division of the Chinese Church between an "official" Church recognized by the government and the "underground" Church, which enjoys no legal protection and is subject to government restriction and harassment. (In practice the line between the two groups is often blurred, but the division is real.) It is difficult to see how these Chinese Catholics could be numbered among the "enemies" of the Holy Father, since Francis has made only a few circumspect comments about the negotiations. Nevertheless, *someone* inside the Vatican seems to be unhappy.

The Vatican's negotiations with China have been secret, and no official stands have been taken except in the most general terms. Why would urging the negotiators to be mindful of the concerns of Chinese Catholics, who have already suffered so much for their faith, be seen as a sign of opposition unless the negotiators were, indeed, prepared to sell out the interests of the underground Church? And why would such cautions be seen as opposition to the *pope*, who has not spoken on the issue and has presumably not been presented with an agreement to approve or reject, unless the negotiators were wrapping themselves in the mantle of papal authority?

Father Bernardo Cervellera, the director of the Church's AsiaNews service, who had served in China before being declared persona non grata there, appeared on the *Vatican Insider* enemies list. Responding with his own essay, "The 'Enemies' of Pope Francis," he defended the attention that his agency had paid to the Catholics who are acting outside the law in China:

> If I were Pope Francis I would appreciate my Cardinals tell-
> ing me about the problems that these Christians suffer who
> are…very much on the peripheries, the face of the suffering
> Christ, part of my flock for which I have to give my life.…
> Unfortunately, Pope Francis has few friends of this caliber.

The pope, Father Cervellera noted, "does not need public defend-ers." Still less did he need supporters who would dismiss all critics as hostile and presume all reservations about papal statements and initia-tives as motivated by hostility. As Father Cervellera wrote in the ring-ing conclusion to his defense, "You can also betray a person with too much applause."

The St. Gallen Mafia

Any powerful leader in any institution runs the risk that he will become the captive of his own Praetorian Guard, the trusted aides who tell him only what he wants to hear (or what they want him to hear) and exclude all discordant voices. For Francis, that danger apparently arose even before his election.

Late in 2015, in an authorized biography of the Belgian cardinal Godfried Danneels, Jürgen Mettepenningen and Karim Schelkens revealed that a cabal of "progressive" cardinals had begun maneuvering for the election of Jorge Bergoglio long before the conclave of 2013. The group had formed years earlier, during the pontificate of John Paul II, to discuss how to resist what they saw as the unhealthy influence of Cardinal Joseph Ratzinger. Along with Danneels, the group included the late Carlo Martini of Milan, the veteran Vatican insider Achille Silvestrini, England's Cormac Murphy-O'Connor, and the Germans Karl Lehmann and Walter Kasper.

Upon the publication of his biography, Danneels referred to this group as a "mafia club," an obviously imprudent choice of words suggesting a sinister conspiracy rather than a simple meeting of like-minded prelates. But the authors of the biography went considerably further, reporting that members of the group—dubbed the "St. Gallen mafia" in reference to the Swiss town where they had met—had worked against Cardinal Ratzinger during the conclave of 2005 and, after their failure to stop his election, began planning a campaign for Bergoglio in the next conclave.

If that report were accurate, it would constitute a major scandal. The rules of papal conclaves include a stern moral injunction against lobbying, and John Paul II had prescribed the penalty of excommunication for any prelate who sought to influence the vote of another cardinal. When the implications of the report were pointed out, Mettepenningen and Schelkens backtracked, saying that they had been misunderstood. The St. Gallen mafia had not formed a lobbying bloc during the 2005 conclave, they now said, and shortly after the election of Benedict XVI the group had stopped meeting.

But if *this* version of the story were accurate, it would really be no story at all. A few cardinals meeting to discuss their shared concerns about Vatican affairs would be an everyday event. Why would the authors bother to mention it? Why would Danneels make his odd, light-hearted reference to a "mafia club"? The authors had worked closely with Danneels, whose presence at the launch party signaled his approval of the work. So it seemed unlikely that the authors had been entirely mistaken about the nature and purpose of the St. Gallen group.

Then more fuel was added to the fire. In a biography of Francis, Austen Ivereigh wrote that Cardinal Murphy-O'Connor, whom Ivereigh once served as a close adviser, had been asked by "progressive" cardinals to sound out Bergoglio about the plan to promote his candidacy at the conclave of 2013. Murphy-O'Connor, who was then above the age of eighty and thus ineligible to participate in a papal election, approached the Argentine cardinal before the conclave and secured his assent to the plan. As Ivereigh reported:

> [I]f he was willing, he said that he believed that at this time of crisis for the Church no cardinal could refuse if asked. Murphy-O'Connor knowingly warned him to "be careful," and that it was his turn now, and was told "capisco"—"I understand."

That "capisco" spoke to the possibility that Bergoglio realized there was a move afoot to promote his election and consented to the campaign—which, again, would have been in grave violation of the canons governing the papal election. And although the campaign may not have been organized by the St. Gallen mafia, the cast of characters—the "progressive" European prelates represented by Cardinal Murphy-O'Connor—looked remarkably similar. With his one-word assent, Cardinal Bergoglio appeared to be putting himself in the hands of the conspirators, indicating that he was prepared to act under their direction.

One other senior prelate spoke openly about his involvement in the St. Gallen campaign. Cardinal Theodore McCarrick, the retired archbishop of Washington, D.C., was also too old to participate in the 2013 conclave, but he did meet with the other cardinals in the "general congregations" that preceded the elections. In a surprisingly candid address to students at Villanova University in October 2013, the elderly cardinal recalled the preparations for the election.

"Before the conclave, nobody thought that there was a chance for Bergoglio," McCarrick told his student audience. But then one evening he received a visit from "a very interesting and influential Italian gentleman," who asked him for a favor. The mysterious guest spoke highly of Bergoglio, said that the Argentine cardinal would bring reforms to the Church, and urged McCarrick, "Talk him up." As he recounted this intriguing story for the Villanova audience, McCarrick said that he had given a noncommittal answer. When his turn came to address the general congregation, however, he urged the election of a cardinal from Latin America.

Maybe there was no active conspiracy or illicit campaign for the election of Bergoglio. Maybe three different cardinals—Danneels, Murphy-O'Connor, and McCarrick—exaggerated their own roles in the process for the sake of a good story. But there can be little doubt that a group of liberal prelates saw the Argentine cardinal as their best hope for changes in the Church. They encouraged his candidacy, and the new pontiff, an outsider now thrust into the top spot at the Vatican, quite understandably would be inclined to look to these same men for advice. Before his election, Bergoglio, an unknown entity in Rome, had not been identified as a leader of the progressive bloc in the College of Cardinals. Now he had emerged from the conclave as the Roman pontiff, and as time passed it became increasingly clear that he intended to carry out the program that was favored by the prelates who had promoted his election.

Intolerance for Criticism

If the newly elected pope saw the members of the St. Gallen mafia as his natural allies, he could also easily be persuaded to see their rivals within the Roman Curia as his rivals too. Within a few months after his election, Francis had moved Cardinal Mauro Piacenza out of his post as the prefect of the Congregation for the Clergy, making him head of the Apostolic Penitentiary, where he would have less influence. Cardinal Raymond Burke, an outspoken defender of tradition who would become the key player in the presentation of the *dubia*, was removed from the Congregation for Bishops—the body that recommends episcopal appointments worldwide—and later from his post as prefect of the Apostolic Signatura. The American cardinal was given the largely ceremonial role of chaplain to the Knights of Malta—and then, months later, even that job was stripped of what little authority it entailed.

Piacenza and Burke at least retained their rank as cardinals. Outside Rome other bishops were removed from office altogether. Within eighteen months of his accession to the See of Peter, Francis had accepted the resignations of Bishops Rogelio Livieres Plano in Paraguay, Mario Oliveri in Italy, Franz-Peter Tebartz-van Elst in Germany, and Robert Finn in the United States. Each of these bishops resigned under fire, having been accused of some form of personal misconduct or administrative malfeasance. But was it a coincidence that they were all perceived as conservatives? John Allen of *Crux* noticed the ideological imbalance in the list of ousted prelates. In a column with the provocative title "Does Pope Francis have an enemies list?" he remarked that even if the pope were merely enforcing Church discipline without regard to the views of the bishops who turned up in his crosshairs, it might be wise to offer an explanation. "Otherwise, the risk is that a good chunk of the Church may conclude that if the pope sees them as the enemy, there's no good reason they shouldn't see him the same way."

Oddly enough, many of Bergoglio's fellow Jesuits once looked upon him as an enemy. Unpopular as the Jesuit provincial in Argentina, he was seen as arbitrary and authoritarian, criticisms that he himself has acknowledged were valid. After his term as provincial, he was given routine assignments—effectively sent into institutional exile—until 1992, when Cardinal Antonio Quarracino of Buenos Aires arranged for him to be appointed an auxiliary bishop. After he became a cardinal and traveled to Rome regularly for meetings, Bergoglio spent little time at Jesuit headquarters. His choice of the name Francis upon his election to the papacy spoke to a Franciscan rather than Jesuit sensibility.

In the papacy, however, Francis soon surrounded himself with Jesuit aides, most notably Antonio Spadaro. Perhaps he felt the need to build strategic alliances to carry out the program of reform that he (and his St. Gallen supporters?) saw as the purpose of his pontificate. He began meeting frequently with Father Adolfo Nicolas, who until 2017 was the superior general of the Jesuits, and he embarked on a program that was certain to please the solidly left-leaning majority within the Society of Jesus.

For a pope bent on change, the Jesuits would be a bulwark. And Francis was bent on change. Father Nicolas recalls that in a conversation about the possibility of yet another papal resignation, Francis told him, "I ask the good Lord to take me once the changes are irreversible." Resistance to such an agenda was inevitable, but Nicholas noted that "for me it was obvious that the criticisms did not remotely bother him."

And yet as the months went on, Francis became increasingly strident, even insulting, in his public utterances. In his homilies at daily Mass, he reproached the "Pharisees," the "doctors of the law," and all who were "rigid" in their interpretation of Church teaching. In language that no one expected from a Roman pontiff, he denounced the "careerist bishop," the "sourpuss," the "smarmy, idolater priest," the "moralistic quibbler," and the "people without light: real downers." Some members of the flock, it became clear, particularly get under the papal skin—the "starched Christian," the "bubble Christian," the "long-faced, mournful funeral Christian," and the "parrot Christian." In a particularly vivid rebuke, he accused journalists who report on conflicts and scandals of "coprophilia" (an "abnormal interest in fecal matter"). Rarely did the pope identify the objects of his ire by name, but from the frequency of his attacks on "rigid" Christians, it seemed clear that he was talking about those who did not accept his calls for change in the Church.

The Gospels' depiction of Christ's frequent confrontations with Pharisees and doctors of the law made them bywords among Christians for sanctimonious legalism, but they are nevertheless important figures in the Jewish tradition. Francis's habitually disparaging use of "Pharisee" and "doctor of the law" eventually drew widely reported protests from an Italian rabbi, Giuseppe Laras, who complained that it belittled the Jewish faith and reflected the influence of Marcionism, a second-century heresy that rejected the Old Testament and denied that the stern God of the Hebrews was the same Deity as the merciful God of the New Testament. Observing that since Vatican II, the Church's official statements have reflected a keen appreciation for the heritage of Judaism, Laras exclaimed, "What a shame that they should be contradicted on a daily basis by the homilies of the Pontiff!"

No one suggested that Francis was actually anti-Semitic, but since he never identified his targets, a wide range of people assumed he was talking about them and took offense. Francis had developed an odd style, emerging as a scold. His rhetoric was radically at odds with his public statements about the need to "accompany" sinners, to tolerate disagreements, to reach out to new constituencies. In his own preaching he hectored his listeners, denouncing more than encouraging.

In a memorable homily delivered in May 2017, Francis argued that an excessive concern with doctrine is a sign of ideology rather than faith. Reflecting on the day's Scripture reading from the Acts of the Apostles, which recounted the debate over enforcing Mosaic Law on Gentile Christians, the pope said that the "liberty of the Spirit" led the disciples to an accord. The dispute, however, he said was caused by "jealousies, power struggles, a certain deviousness that wanted to profit from and to buy power," temptations against which the Church must always guard.

The disciples who insisted on the enforcement of Mosaic Law, the pope said, were "fanatics." They "were not believers; they were ideologized." Thus he appeared to suggest that the early Church leaders who disagreed with St. Paul on the enforcement of Mosaic Law—including St. James and, before the Council of Jerusalem, which settled the question, even St. Peter himself—"were not believers." The Scriptural account of that council offers no evidence that those on opposite sides of the question rendered harsh judgments of one other. They met, argued vigorously over a point that was not yet clear, and with the help of the Holy Spirit reached a decision that resolved their differences. Francis acknowledged that it is "a duty of the Church to clarify doctrine," as the apostles did at the Council of Jerusalem. But he did not acknowledge that his critics within the hierarchy were calling for precisely the same sort of clarification with respect to papal teaching on marriage and the Eucharist.

A Troubled Personality?

During his visit to the United States in 2015, in an address to the country's bishops, Pope Francis said:

> Harsh and divisive language does not befit the tongue of a pastor, it has no place in his heart; although it may momentarily seem to win the day, only the enduring allure of goodness and love remains truly convincing.

That sentence encapsulates Francis's consistent advice to Church leaders: a plea for compassion, tolerance, willingness to listen, and reluctance to pass judgment. And the popular perception is that the pope is just that sort of prelate: kind, soft-spoken, avuncular, uniting rather than dividing. Yet even a cursory reading of the pope's daily homilies reveals harsh rhetoric, stinging rebukes, and angry denunciations such as we have not heard from a Roman pontiff for generations.

Is this sort of preaching, with its emphasis on the negative and its intolerance toward opposition, a sign of a troubled or at least intemperate personality? Francis has admitted to interviewers that he is impulsive by nature. And his management style confirms that appraisal. In a moment of unusual candor, the former spokesman for the pope, Father Federico Lombardi, acknowledged that problem in July 2015. "No one knows all of what he's doing," Lombardi said. "His personal secretary doesn't even know. I have to call around: One person knows one part of his schedule, someone else knows another part." In other words, there is no clear organization of the papal schedule. Francis stirs up confusion, if not chaos, for his staff. How could this be explained? Is it evidence of the pope's personal disorder? Or has he found himself out of his depth? The latter hypothesis might help to explain why the pope has come to rely heavily on his circle of trusted allies while showing dwindling tolerance for clear and candid criticism.

From early in his pontificate, Francis showed no patience with officials of the Roman Curia who questioned his policies. As tensions heightened, morale plummeted in Vatican offices. Reports circulated in the Italian media—too many to be ignored—of staff members called before the pope for reprimands because of unguarded remarks in private conversations. The pope demanded the immediate dismissal of three clerics on the staff of the Congregation for the Doctrine of the Faith, angrily refusing to give an explanation and insisting that he had the authority to insist on obedience. Psychologists began quietly to speculate that the pope's frequent displays of agitation pointed to some personal unrest.

Even as he denounced his critics, Francis continued to tell interviewers that he was not bothered at all by criticism—indeed that he welcomed honest disagreements. Here, too, the gap between the pope's actions and his public statements prompted questions. Was he refusing to acknowledge the reality of his situation? Was he lapsing into the authoritarian mode that had marked his tenure as a Jesuit provincial? Was he living with some special tension about his role as successor to St. Peter—or perhaps with conflicts of longer duration?

In a revealing book-length interview published in September 2017, Francis disclosed to the French sociologist Dominique Wolton that he had met weekly with a psychoanalyst for six months when he was forty-two years old. The sessions "helped me a lot at a moment in my life," the pope said, adding that at the time he "needed to clarify things." Perhaps not surprisingly, those sessions with the psychoanalyst took place toward the end of his troubled term as Jesuit provincial in Argentina. Francis told Wolton that he no longer suffered from the anxiety that led him to seek help, but he did say that he had declined to live in the apostolic palace "for psychiatric reasons." He told the interviewer: "I can't live alone, do you understand?"

As a young priest, Father Bergoglio had taken a perverse pleasure in shocking pious Catholics. Two nephews testified that when they were very young, their uncle Jorge had encouraged them to use profanity, to the distress of their parents. His sister recalled that once, when Father Bergoglio was preaching at Mass, his little nephew burst out with "a very bad word," and the future pope "could not stop laughing."

Maybe those incidents could be written off as the indiscretion of youth, but Bergoglio was fully mature—in fact, he was the Vicar of Christ—when he discouraged another young boy from a show of piety. Matthew Schmitz recounts the incident for *First Things*:

> He was making a visit to the Vatican grottos, under whose vaults his various predecessors, saint and heretic, Peter and Honorius, are laid out alike. With cameras rolling, he paused to greet the attendants who waited at the entrance. There he noticed an altar boy who had his hands clasped in an attitude of reverence. Francis began to tease him: "Are your hands bound together? It looks like they're stuck," he said as he pulled them apart. As Francis went down into the tombs, the boy put his hands back together.

Could there be some internal conflict that would account for the pope's intolerance of criticism and his impatience with piety? Did his disgust with "doctors of the law" betray his own unresolved tensions with the laws of the Church? One potential answer to those questions, interestingly enough, is related to his being the first Jesuit pope.

When a Jesuit makes his solemn profession, he pledges that he will neither seek *nor accept* any position of authority in the Church unless he is ordered under obedience to do so. This vow, instituted to allay fears that the Society of Jesus was scheming for control, is at least a theoretical obstacle for any Jesuit to accept an appointment as a bishop. But Jesuits also pledge obedience to the Roman pontiff, so when the pope asks a Jesuit priest to become a bishop, the priest might take it for granted that he is called to that post under obedience. In any case, scores of Jesuits, like Father Bergoglio, have accepted episcopal appointments, presumably on that basis.

Once he becomes a bishop, a Jesuit is partially released from his vow of obedience, and he is no longer answerable to his Jesuit superior for his decisions *as a bishop.* So a Jesuit cardinal is under no obligation to follow his provincial's wishes when he votes in a papal conclave. But Bergoglio's position as a Jesuit who was *elected* at a conclave was entirely unprecedented. He had sworn, years earlier, that he would not accept advancement except under obedience. Now he was offered advancement, but since he was not answerable to any Jesuit superior and there was no reigning pontiff to command him, he was not under obedience. He resolved the conundrum by accepting election, obviously—perhaps reasoning that the vote of the conclave was an indication of God's will, which he should obey. But could there be lingering questions in his mind, or on his conscience, about that decision, contributing to the tensions that he has displayed?

"Airport Bishops" and the "Smell of the Sheep"

Whether it is an odd administrative style or a quirk of personality that makes Francis so hard on his critics, it cannot be denied that he is loyal to his allies. In fact, it has become apparent that this pope selects his associates on the basis of personal loyalty rather than theological acumen or pastoral performance. Among the prelates he has chosen as his closest advisers, several have displayed characteristics that he has roundly denounced in his public statements.

Take for instance the leaders of the Council of Cardinals, which he established to advise him on Vatican reforms. The man appointed coordinator of this influential group is the Honduran cardinal Oscar Rodríguez Maradiaga, who once dismissed sex-abuse complaints against the clergy as a creation of the American media—which, he observed, were disproportionately controlled by Jewish interests. (He later apologized for that remark.) After a coup in Honduras in 2009, Maradiaga opened up divisions in the Church by vocally supporting the new regime—"democratic institutions are in place," he declared—even as the Organization of American States imposed sanctions on the country, and the leaders of the Dominican and Jesuit orders in Honduras agreed that the coup was unconstitutional.

Cardinal Maradiaga has not been a conspicuously successful pastor at home. When he was appointed archbishop of Tegucigalpa in 1993, Honduras was more than 75 percent Catholic. Today Catholics are less than 50 percent of the population. With a violent crime rate roughly ten times that of Chicago and five times that of the Democratic Republic of Congo and the Central African Republic (two countries in the grip of civil war), Honduras is a nation desperately in need of spiritual leadership. Yet Maradiaga has been the epitome of the "airport bishop" that Francis denounces, jetting around the world to deliver speeches rather than tending to his flock.

Ensconced as the head of the Vatican's new center of power, Maradiaga was quick to display his loyalty to Francis by denigrating those perceived as opponents of the pope's agenda. Questioned about the four cardinals who submitted the *dubia*, he replied, "I think, in the first place, that they have not read *Amoris laetitia*, because unfortunately that is the truth." Mocking the four cardinals as "already in retirement," he accused them of indulging in "a new Pharisaism" and of presuming "that they are in charge of the Church's doctrine." And with swagger bordering on hubris, Maradiaga announced the grand plan for the pontificate: "The Pope wants to take this Church renewal to the point where it becomes irreversible."

The Honduran prelate expressed his contempt for the pope's critics even more brazenly in a book-length interview, published in 2017, that features a stunning personal attack on Cardinal Raymond Burke. He dismisses the American as "a poor man" whose thoughts "don't merit further comment," and charges Burke with fomenting dissent by asking questions about *Amoris Laetitia*. "What senses does it make to publish writings against the Pope?" Maradiaga asks, attributing Burke's concerns to frustrated ambition: "The cardinal who sustains this is a disappointed man, in that he wanted power and lost it."

Another key member of the Council of Cardinals, Reinhard Marx of Munich, the president of the German bishops' conference, has, like Maradiaga, presided over the collapse of the Church in his own diocese. The Catholic population that Marx leads has declined by nearly one hundred thousand since his appointment in 2007, and his archdiocese had *one* new candidate for the priesthood in 2017.

Still, there is another, more compelling reason to be concerned about Cardinal Marx's perspective. "There is always a danger of corruption within the Church," Francis warned visiting German bishops in November 2015. "This happens when the Church, instead of being devoted to faith in our Lord, in the Prince of Peace, in joy, in salvation, becomes dominated by money and power." Nowhere else does the Catholic Church have so much money, so much power, and—is this surprising?—such a precarious future as in Germany.

Francis longs for "a Church that is poor, and for the poor." He would not find that Church in Germany. If a German citizen is registered as a member of a religious congregation, the government collects a "church tax" from him—a surcharge on his regular income tax that is passed along to the church in which he is registered. The tax has made the Catholic Church in Germany enormously wealthy, but that wealth comes directly from the government and only indirectly from the faithful. The potential for corruption—for bending Church policies to ensure smooth dealings with the government—is obvious.

And to say that the Church's funds come indirectly from the "faithful" is to use that term loosely. Anyone who is registered as a church member, whether or not he ever shows up, pays the church tax. The Catholic Church's income, therefore, depends on the number of Germans registered as Catholic. If that number drops, so does the Church's income. Bishops, therefore, look askance at Catholics who do not register their church affiliation. The German hierarchy has even moved to deny the Sacraments to unregistered Catholics.

Strong-arming the faithful to register, and thus pay up, may contradict the German bishops' public pleas for a "welcoming" Church, but it is the result of a mass exodus from the pews. In the 1960s, about 50 percent of the country's registered Catholics were at Mass on any given Sunday; today that figure is 10 percent. With the church tax creeping upward, inactive Catholics have realized that they can save money by removing themselves from the list of registered Catholics. Each year since 2012, more than one hundred thousand German Catholics have taken that step.

Nevertheless, the financial wealth of the Church in Germany remains enormous. The church tax brings in more than five billion euros each year, and the revenue trend is upward. That enormous income allows the German hierarchy to sponsor a wide range of medical, educational, and social programs. In fact the Catholic Church is the country's second-largest employer, behind only the government.

The German hierarchy is struggling to maintain an empire of social services while the ranks of the faithful dwindle. Is it any wonder, then, that the German hierarchy has taken the lead in calling for a relaxation of Church discipline? The German bishops have argued that the Church should show a merciful attitude toward homosexual Catholics, divorced Catholics, feminist Catholics. Are these calls motivated by an honest desire to draw everyone closer to God or by a financial incentive to keep people on the parish rolls? In the German

Church, it can be difficult to distinguish between the merciful and the mercenary.

The Dismissal of Cardinal Müller

Late in June 2017, a rumor began to circulate in Rome that the pope planned to remove another German prelate, Cardinal Gerhard Müller, from his post as prefect of the Congregation for the Doctrine of the Faith. Appointed by Benedict XVI, Müller had been generally regarded as a conservative presence at the Vatican, most notably when he insisted that "*Amoris laetitia* must clearly be interpreted in the light of the whole doctrine of the Church." His personal relationship with Francis had not been warm, his influence had declined notably, and his five-year term as prefect, which ordinarily would be renewed as a matter of course, would expire on July 2.

The rumor proved correct. On the last day of his term, having received no prior indication that his appointment would not be renewed and in circumstances that seemed calculated to humiliate him, Müller was brusquely informed that his tenure as prefect had ended. The pope offered no explanation for his removal and declined to tell him who his replacement would be. (It was Archbishop Luis Ladaria Ferrer, a Spanish Jesuit who had been serving as Müller's immediate subordinate.)

As head of the Vatican congregation charged with preserving the integrity of Catholic doctrine, Cardinal Müller had been caught in the middle of the debate over *Amoris Laetitia*. After expressing his misgivings about the Kasper proposal—which the pope ignored—he played the loyal soldier, insisting that the document was fully orthodox. Although he had voiced dismay over the differing interpretations of the apostolic exhortation, insisting that the teaching of the universal Church could not vary from one diocese to another, he pointedly declined to give his public endorsement to the call for a papal clarification. Apparently his balancing act did not satisfy Francis.

Even after his rude dismissal, Müller continued to defend the pope, insisting—against all evidence—that his departure was a matter of administrative routine rather than ideological incompatibility. "There were no differences between me and Pope Francis," he told the *Allgemeine Zeitung* of Mainz. The pontiff had decided to end the practice of routinely extending Vatican appointments, he said, and "I happened to be the first one to which this applied." (Three other prominent Vatican officials had completed their five-year appointments in the past few months, and all three had remained in place.) A few days later, however, still proclaiming that he was "always loyal to the pope and always will be," Müller did criticize the shabby way he had been treated: "I cannot accept this way of doing things." Recalling Francis's earlier firings of clerics on the CDF staff, Müller said that Church leaders should be bound by the precepts of Catholic social teaching in treating their employees with dignity.

In the dismissal of Cardinal Müller, there was a striking reversal of roles. It was not the stern German "inquisitor general" but the smiling Argentine pope—supposedly the embodiment of mercy and compassion—who demanded unquestioning acquiescence to his authority. Once again the pope's actions were at variance with his words.

Breaking Down Pockets of Resistance

Another revealing personnel move, a few steps lower in the Vatican's organization chart, was the appointment of Archbishop Vincenzo Paglia as president of the Pontifical Academy for Life. As the name suggests, the academy had been a bulwark of the world's pro-life and pro-family movements since it was established by John Paul II in 1994. As such, the office was an outpost of opposition to the progressive Catholic leaders who sought to remove the Church from the front lines of the "culture wars." Now that profile was to change.

For anyone devoted to the Catholic vision of marriage and the family, Paglia's record was troubling. He was responsible for a shocking sex-education guide that featured explicit images, instructed young children in sexual techniques, and encouraged discussion of sexuality without reference to the Church's moral teaching. Paglia had also hosted a series of seminars leading up to the Synod on the Family that were heavily tilted in favor of the Kasper proposal. He had eulogized Marco Pannella, an Italian politician who had led the fight for legal divorce and abortion, calling him "a man of great spirituality" and "an inspirer of a nicer life for this world," whose death was "a great loss for this country."

The *LifeSite News* service in Canada later revealed that while bishop of Terni-Narni-Amelia, Italy, Paglia had commissioned an enormous homoerotic mural for the cathedral. Among the figures in this bizarre painting—one in a netful of writhing nudes—is the bishop himself, complete with his episcopal zucchetto.

Paglia's papal marching orders in his new post were to focus on "the new challenges concerning the value of life." The pope elaborated:

> I refer to the various aspects concerning the care of the dignity of the human person in the various ages of existence, mutual respect between genders and generations, the defense of the dignity of every single human being, the promotion of quality of human life that integrates the material and spiritual values, in view of an authentic 'human ecology', which helps to restore the original balance of creation between the human person and the whole universe.

Conspicuously missing from the Holy Father's list of concerns were abortion, euthanasia, divorce, and contraception, concerns that had been priorities during the pontificate of John Paul II. Their absence was particularly noticeable to American Catholics, since the papal directives coincided with the disclosure that abortion clinics were selling fetal tissue for profit, a grisly illustration of the "culture of death" against which John Paul II had warned. Evidently the Pontifical Academy for Life was being redirected.

A new direction called for new personnel as well. Early in 2017, the Vatican announced that the Pontifical Academy for Life had postponed its annual assembly. It gradually came to light that the postponement was necessary because the academy had no members other than its new president. The entire membership had been purged. The original plan for the annual assembly had been to focus on *Donum Vitae*, the Congregation for the Doctrine of the Faith's 1987 instruction on artificial procreation. That topic was discarded, replaced by the blander "Accompanying Life: New Responsibilities in the Technological Era."

Outside the confines of the Vatican, Francis put his stamp on the Italian bishops' conference by naming Nunzio Galantino as secretary general, giving him a prominent voice in Italian public affairs. He promptly showed his true colors by declaring that he could not "identify with the expressionless person who stands outside the abortion clinic reciting the Rosary." Even before the Synod for the Family took up the discussion of the Kasper proposal, Galantino announced that in his view, couples in "irregular matrimonial situations" should not be excluded from Communion, maintaining that the Church's perennial policy was "an unjustified price to pay, in addition to de facto discrimination."

Galantino's public statements and the gutting of the Pontifical Academy for Life left many thousands of dedicated Catholics feeling betrayed. After years of faithful battle against the culture of death, inspired by the steady support of the Vicar of Christ, they were suddenly receiving rebukes rather than encouragement from Rome. Galantino told the world that he could not identify with pro-life activists, and the activists in turn could not identify with the new policies of the Vatican under Francis.

American Conservatism and the "Ecumenism of Hate"

In the United States, conservative Catholics have long been the papacy's natural and most enthusiastic supporters. Although their views have diverged from those of the popes on certain prudential questions, they have been allied on most of the defining cultural and moral issues of the past fifty years. They began to suspect early in Francis's papacy that the goodwill they had enjoyed under John Paul II and Benedict XVI was diminished, but in July 2017 it became unmistakably clear that Rome's goodwill has turned into antipathy when *La Civiltà Cattolica* published a harsh denunciation of American conservatives.

The essay, written by the now-notorious Antonio Spadaro, S.J., and Marcelo Figueroa, a Presbyterian pastor whom Bergoglio befriended in Buenos Aires, betrays profound confusion about its subject, the role of conservative Catholics and evangelicals in American politics. According to Spadaro and Figueroa, these two malign forces, sharing a Manichaean view of a world divided into absolute good and absolute evil, have joined in an "ecumenism of hate," pursuing a "[t]riumphalist, arrogant and vindictive ethnicism [that] is actually the opposite of Christianity."

The ignorance and intemperance of this venomous essay are doubly troublesome because the authors' closeness to Francis and the semi-official standing of *La Civiltà Cattolica* raise the presumption that it reflects the pope's own thinking.

Embracing a Secular Agenda

The peremptory dismissal of Müller, the ascendancy of Maradiaga and Galantino, the bitter partisan tone adopted by Spadaro and Figueroa—all exemplified the new direction of this pontificate: moving away from an emphasis on the dignity of life and the integrity of the family, embracing instead the more popular causes of secular liberalism. The Vatican began to organize conferences on immigration reform and climate change. Twice Francis hosted meetings of "popular movements," with invitations going out to environmental activists, ethnic separatists, militant feminists, and community organizers—but not to pro-life leaders or defenders of traditional marriage.

When he was asked why a Vatican conference on climate change had not included speakers who questioned the popular consensus, Bishop Marcelo Sánchez Sorondo, the chancellor of the Pontifical Academy of Social Sciences, angrily rebuked the reporter who posed the question. There were *no* respectable scientists, he insisted, who would dispute the prevailing belief that human actions cause climate change. Comparing the pope's teaching on global warming to the Church's teaching on abortion, Sánchez Sorondo said the "judgement must be considered magisterial—it is not an opinion." Father Joseph Fessio, S.J., the founder of Ignatius Press, replied, in an interview with *LifeSite News*: "Neither the Pope nor Bishop Sorondo can speak on a matter of science with any binding authority, so to use the word 'magisterium' in both cases is equivocal at best, and ignorant in any case." Fessio added, "To equate a papal position on abortion with a position on global warming is worse than wrong; it is an embarrassment for the Church."

Yet Sánchez Sorondo went even further. In an exchange with Stefano Gennarini of the Center for Family and Human Rights, he claimed that the only opposition to the theory of human-induced global warming arose from the Tea Party movement, adding that any scientists who raised questions about the theory were being paid by the oil industry. He went on to deny that the United Nations, which had been heavily involved in the climate-change conference, has played a role in promoting abortion and contraception. In an interview some months later, he added that climate change is the main cause for the world's migration crisis. On all of these points—which are matters of fact, not opinion—the bumptious Sánchez Sorondo was demonstrably wrong. But his style of debate, featuring an attack on the integrity of his opponents, bore the familiar stamp of this pontificate.

A Lawmaker Who Ignores the Law

And what is the stamp of the pontificate? Clearly Francis is bent on bringing change to the Church and is impatient with resistance to that change. He betrays his impatience with rules that stand in his way—even, curiously enough, when he has the undoubted authority to change those rules.

For some time, Catholic liturgists debated about a ceremony within the ritual for Holy Thursday in which the priest-celebrant washes the feet of several members of the congregation, imitating Jesus' gesture of humility and love for his apostles at the Last Supper. Traditionally, only men were included in this ritual, since it evokes the memory of the apostles, who were all male, and the institution of the priesthood, which is reserved to males. But in recent years some Catholics had argued that the benefits of including women outweighed the importance of that symbolism. At the time when Francis was elected, the Church's official liturgical directives sided with tradition; only males were to be included. Francis had the authority to change those rules. Instead, at the first Holy Thursday ceremony after his installation as Roman pontiff, he simply ignored the liturgical directives and included women in the papal foot-washing ritual. Only later did he issue a liturgical directive, changing the rule that he had flouted.

Similarly, in November 2016 the pope announced that he was extending to all Catholic priests the authority to absolve the sin of procuring an abortion. Previously, the Code of Canon Law provided that anyone directly involved in procuring an abortion was subject to the penalty of excommunication. Under the new dispensation granted by Francis, the sin could be absolved by any priest in a sacramental confession.[1] At a press conference introducing the new policy, Archbishop Rino Fisichella explained that the pope had changed the relevant section of canon law. He had *not* actually amended the law, however; the language was still on the books. That was a technicality, the archbishop argued: "Canon law is a body of laws, and whenever the

---

1 Canon lawyers argued that the penalty of excommunication applied only to those who procured an abortion in full knowledge that they would be excommunicated for doing so. Persons ignorant of the canonical rule who were involved in an abortion could be absolved in an ordinary confession. The pope's new directive did not apply to them.

Pope introduces a measure that alters the dictates of the law, the article that specific measure concerns, necessarily needs to be changed." Indeed, there was a need to bring the law into conformity with the pope's directive. As the supreme legislator for the Church, the pope had the power to make that change, but he did not. He left the law on the books, and established a policy that contravened it.

Nor was this simply a case in which the alteration in the Code of Canon Law lagged a bit behind the papal directive. A full year earlier, as the Jubilee Year of Mercy began, Francis had given a special group of priests, the Missionaries of Mercy, the authority to absolve sins of abortion. So the pope's policy and the language of canon law had been in conflict for months.

Furthermore, a Catholic who is excommunicated is barred from the Sacraments, including the Sacrament of Penance. So although a priest could absolve the sin in a confession, a woman who had procured an abortion and knew that she had thereby incurred excommunication would not be able to make a sacramental confession. Fortunately in most cases, Catholic women who regret having abortions are unaware that they have been subject to excommunication, so they do not hesitate to approach the Sacrament and seek absolution. But then other women, who had sought and received absolution long ago, unaware of the canonical penalty, might now wonder where they stood. Were they still excommunicated? Was the absolution valid?

In short, the pope's failure to synchronize canon law with his new policy risked widespread confusion and distress. One vexed priest, commenting on the change, remarked, "Over the next few months I expect we'll be spending a good deal of time in the confessional explaining the Church's teaching to aged women who have had the sin actually forgiven years ago."

The pope's tendency to ignore rules rather than change them played out in a much less serious way when he gave a group of activists permission to grow crops on a plot of land on the outskirts of Rome owned by the Vatican. Francis gave his blessing to a project initiated by Omero Lauri, a proponent of squatters' rights, who asserted: "We believe that all people have the right to a piece of land for free." Lauri met with the pontiff and secured his permission only after having occupied the land, but he reported that Francis supported his movement. Still the pope did not give Lauri and his cohort any legal title to the land. Police cited the squatters for setting up an illegal café on the property, serving food without a license on property they did not own. And owners of other properties in the neighborhood looked askance at the little cooperative, wondering whether the squatters would move in on their land as well. Once again the pope could have avoided the complications by granting legal title to the cooperative, but he seemed quite content to flout the rules and live with the confusion—to "make a mess," as he had encouraged young people.

Packing the College of Cardinals

On one point, however, Francis has acted quite deliberately and methodically. He has been careful to appoint cardinals who support his views, increasing the likelihood that when his pontificate comes to an end, the man they elect will continue his policies. This is perhaps the most important facet of his plan to make the changes in the Church "irreversible."

In a syndicated column from early 2017, the American scholar George Weigel punctures the myth, popular in liberal circles, that Popes John Paul II and Benedict XVI had imposed ideological control over the Vatican. Those pontiffs, Weigel points out, regularly promoted men with dramatically different theological outlooks to the College of Cardinals, bestowing red hats on Cardinals Kasper, Marx, Daneels, McCarrick, and yes, Bergoglio. The same cannot be said of Francis. He has elevated his potential allies in preference to more senior prelates whose approach does not match his own. From the American archbishops who might have been considered for membership of the College of Cardinals in 2017, Francis chose two notably liberal prelates:

Blase Cupich of Chicago and Joseph Tobin of Indianapolis (who was immediately moved to Newark, closer to America's media center). He passed over some of the country's most prominent Catholic leaders: Archbishops José Gómez of Los Angeles, the leader of the country's largest diocese, who would have been the first Hispanic cardinal in U.S. history; Charles Chaput of Philadelphia, a thoughtful and articulate defender of the natural law; and William Lori of Baltimore (the oldest American diocese), who was the point man for the American hierarchy in the battle to preserve religious freedom against the encroachment of government regulation.

The pope—any pope—has every right to elevate his own men to the College of Cardinals. The way he exercises that right, however, reveals a great deal about how he understands his role as leader of the universal Church.

To qualify for the College of Cardinals, a prelate should show an unassailable character, a firm commitment to the established doctrines of the Church, and a willingness—signified by his scarlet garments—to shed his blood, if necessary, in defense of the Faith. Beyond that, how should the pope make his selections?

The College of Cardinals has two main functions: to act as a circle of advisers for the pope and, when the time comes, to elect his successor. For each of those purposes, a prudent pontiff draws on the diverse resources of the universal Church, appointing cardinals with different backgrounds and different viewpoints. Ideally, when they meet in conclave, the cardinals should represent all of the world's faithful Catholics, with their many different cares and concerns.

During the past century, Roman pontiffs have made a deliberate effort to give the College of Cardinals a more international flavor, recognizing that the Holy Spirit might have something special to say to the universal Church through the voices of Catholic leaders from Africa or Asia. By expanding the membership of the College beyond Europe, the pope provides more room for the Spirit to speak to his

Church. At the same time, by restricting membership, the pope could restrict the movement of the Spirit. Francis has followed the trend toward internationalization of the College, but he has restricted his choices in another way, showing a strong preference for prelates who share his own perspective on the Church's pastoral priorities.

John Paul II and Benedict XVI took a much more conventional approach. They chose new cardinals primarily from among the archbishops of the world's most important archdioceses, or from the leadership of the Roman Curia. (Their few unconventional choices were, as a rule, over the age of eighty, for whom the red hat was a recognition of their past service to the Church; because of their age, these cardinals would not be eligible to participate in a papal election.) They obviously did *not* exclude prelates who had different theological perspectives.

And was that not a much wiser approach? If the pope seeks sound advice from his cardinals, he must hear from men who will challenge his way of thinking. A humble pontiff will guard against the temptation to think that his perspective is the only valid Catholic perspective. He will realize, too, that even if his policies are right for the Church today, the Church of the future might need different policies.

The Roman pontiff is—or should be—the focus of unity in the Church. John XXIII once remarked that as universal pastor, he was responsible for *all* Catholics, including both those who had their foot on the gas and those who had their foot on the brake. Francis clearly has his foot on the gas. But insofar as he is ignoring and excluding prelates who have their feet on the brake—and who would urge him to do the same—he is risking a crack-up.

One staunch ally of Francis, the liberal Jesuit Thomas Reese, writing in the *National Catholic Reporter*, acknowledges that the pope's selections for the College of Cardinals are "the most revolutionary thing Francis has done in terms of Church governance." Having played the role of activist within the Church for years, Reese recognizes that an arbitrary exercise of power by Francis today could justify an equally arbitrary action by some future pontiff who might have different ideas. If John Paul II or Benedict XVI had taken a similar approach to naming new cardinals, writes Reese, "Frankly, I would have been outraged."

CHAPTER EIGHT

Tradition in the Balance

I n the aftermath of the Second Vatican Council, the Catholic Church was torn by disputes about liturgy and morality, disputes that were not confined to theological faculties, but reached into parishes and family homes. Scores of books have been written about the council and its consequences, and I do not propose to add to that literature. I simply want to make the point that in the late 1960s and through the 1970s, the Catholic Church was sorely divided.

The conflict involved irreconcilable interpretations of the council's mandate. Liberal or "progressive" Catholics believed not only that Vatican II had wrought profound changes in the Church but that the "spirit of Vatican II" would extend the era change far into the future, overthrowing old dogmas and disciplines. Conservative Catholics argued that this liberal vision was a misinterpretation of the council and that the radical changes sweeping through the Church went beyond anything authorized in the documents of the council. A third group, traditionalist Catholics, tacitly agreed with the liberals that the council had made radical changes in Catholic teaching, but they insisted that these changes must be reversed.

Continuing for a generation, this conflict severely strained the unity of the Church. Every tenet of Catholic doctrine was assailed. The liturgy was transformed almost beyond recognition. A clear sense of Catholic identity was lost. Thousands of the faithful, lacking clear guidance, drifted away from the Church. Even among those who remained, the fault lines became increasingly evident. Catholics began to choose their parishes according to the style of the liturgy or the content of the preaching; the differences from parish to parish and from diocese to diocese could make a visitor wonder whether these churches were still united by the same faith.

That sort of turmoil was not entirely new to the Catholic world. In the history of the Church, major councils have frequently been followed by periods of confusion until the new teachings have been absorbed. But Vatican II was the first ecumenical council in the age of modern communications, when every new theological argument was instantaneously disseminated throughout the world. Ordinary Catholics, as well as interested observers outside the Church, could develop their own views about the conciliar debates. Those views, however, were strongly influenced by the secular media, which were nearly unanimous in decreeing that the liberal or "progressive" wing of the Church had the better of the debates.

In *Turmoil and Truth*, the British Catholic author Philip Trower explains the public perception of the post-conciliar Church with this vivid image:

> Six men are pushing a heavily loaded car which has run out of fuel. Three of them, who have been riding in the car, want to push it 20 yards to get it into a lay-by. The other three, who have offered to help, mean to push the car 50 yards and shove it over a cliff followed by the car owner and his two friends. Once the pushing begins and the car starts moving it is probable the car is going to come to rest more than 20 yards from the starting point even if it does not end up at the cliff's foot.
>
> Now let us imagine what a group of people watching from a nearby hilltop will make of the incident. They will

start by assuming that all six men have the same intentions. The car is moving steadily forward. Then they see three of the men detach themselves from the back of the car, run around to the front and try to stop it. Which are the trouble-makers? Those surely who are now opposing the process that has been started.

Needless to say, this analogy is imperfect. The Catholic Faith was not "out of gas" before Vatican II, and it would be unfair to imply that everyone calling for radical change was motivated by a desire to destroy the Church. But Trower makes the important point that, like the three men in the car, the Church was on a journey before the battle began, and to understand the battle one must understand that journey.

John Paul II and the Restoration

During the long pontificate of St. John Paul II, the turmoil within the Church slowly subsided. No one could accuse the Polish pontiff of opposing the council's teachings. He had been an active and influential participant at Vatican II, and his pastoral leadership of the archdiocese of Krakow was widely regarded as a model for the proper implementation of the council's teachings. Nevertheless, he rejected the excesses that had been promoted by some of the overzealous champions of reform. Thanks also to his enormous popularity and his deserved reputation for personal holiness, he held the confidence of the faithful and was able to steer the universal Church back toward normalcy.

John Paul II faced resistance, to be sure, and a good deal of it came from within the Society of Jesus. In their eye-opening book *Passionate Uncertainty: Inside the American Jesuits*, Peter McDonough and Eugene Bianchi take a sympathetic look at the progressive Jesuits who were appalled by the Polish pope's refusal to change Church doctrine, particularly on issues of sexuality. "He's not one of the worst popes;

he's the worst," one Jesuit told the authors. "I am appalled by the direction of the present papacy," said another. "I am scandalized by Rome's intransigent refusal to re-examine its doctrines regarding gender and sex," said another. One Jesuit made a shocking statement of disloyalty: "The Church as we know it is dying. I hope and pray that the Society [of Jesus] will help to facilitate this death and resurrection." Another, in more measured tones, boasted: "The society has not sold its soul to the 'restoration' of John Paul II."

That restoration continued under Benedict XVI, who had been John Paul's right-hand man. Helping to settle the lingering confusion about the proper interpretation of Vatican II, he explained that Catholic doctrine and discipline should always be seen in continuity with the centuries of the Church's tradition. The Faith does not change, though over time the Church refines her understanding of truths that have been known from the days of the apostles. Vatican II, Benedict explained, did not, and could not, constitute a break with Catholic tradition. Proposing a "hermeneutic of continuity," by which the teachings of Vatican II were to be read in the light of the teachings of previous councils and magisterial statements, he rejected the extremism of both the radicals and the traditionalists, who agreed that Vatican II had repudiated previous Church teachings—the former welcoming the rupture and the latter loathing it.

John Paul II and Benedict XVI did not repair all the fissures in the structure of the Church that appeared after Vatican II. Far from it. For ordinary Catholics, the problems persisted at the parish level, where liturgical abuses continued and religious education was shallow. Catholics seeking a reverent liturgy had to shop for a congenial parish, often far from their homes, and parents determined to educate their children in the Faith hunted out the few rigorous parish programs or, more and more often, taught their children at home. Still, these struggling Catholics knew that in parochial conflicts, they could cite recent papal documents, confident that they had the support of the Vatican.

"Irreversible" Change

No longer. Francis has reopened the debate about the continuity of Catholic teaching. His supporters see him as the liberator of the spirit of Vatican II, bringing permanent change to the Church, while his critics protest that the Church cannot alter its fundamental doctrine. So the intramural disputes that split dioceses and parishes and families a generation ago are flaring up once again. Orthodox Catholics who thought they could finally foresee the restoration of reverence and beauty in the liturgy and of serious substance in catechesis see their hard-won gains slipping away. That conflict in itself would be cause for alarm. But there is more.

As the pope's closest advisers have stated on several occasions, Francis intends not only to change the Church but to lock in the changes. Archbishop Victor Fernández, a fellow Argentine who helped the pontiff draft his first encyclical, remarked in 2015, "You have to realize that he is aiming at reform that is irreversible."

For Catholics who have weathered two generations of confusion and conflict, clinging to beliefs they hold precious, the prospect of "irreversible change" along the lines suggested by Fernández is horrifying. The unsettling "Francis effect" has left thousands of Catholics constantly anxious, easily rattled by the latest rumors from Rome.

In the spring of 2017, for example, a report circulated that the pope had authorized a Vatican commission to reconsider the teaching of *Humanae Vitae,* the 1968 encyclical of Paul VI reaffirming the Church's age-old condemnation of contraception that had touched off the bitterest theological disputes of recent decades. The report was not quite accurate, but the reality was unsettling enough. It was not the pope himself who was reopening the question—at least not directly. The Pontifical John Paul II Institute for Studies on Marriage and Family (named after the most eloquent defender of *Humanae Vitae*) was sponsoring a "study group," working under the auspices of the recently remodeled Pontifical Academy for Life, to examine the history of the preparation of the encyclical. A pontifical institute would not undertake a reevaluation of a papal encyclical unless the sponsors were confident that the pope would approve. Since the members of the study group were known for their lack of enthusiasm for the Church's teaching on contraception, veterans of the battles over *Humanae Vitae* were hardly paranoid in fearing that the ugly controversy could erupt again—this time with the Vatican supporting the critics of constant Catholic teaching.

Far from employing the "hermeneutic of continuity," Francis has often displayed a dismissive, almost sneering, attitude toward Church leaders of the past. In an address to Jesuit officials in October 2016, he said that the missionary work of the early Jesuits was marred by "a hegemonic conception of Roman centralism." A Catholic historian, Bronwen Catherine McShea, takes exception to that phrase, which seems to "dismiss, and gratuitously to tarnish the memory of, Church leaders of the distant past for the sake of advancing a current agenda for inculturated forms of Christianity among the world's indigenous cultures."

McShea is also dismayed by the pope's remark to a Lutheran delegation from Finland: "The intention of Martin Luther five hundred years ago was to renew the Church, not divide her." On the contrary, McShea writes, "from early on, Luther's Reformation was centrally about separating, promptly—with the help of powerful territorial princes and city magistrates with local influence and armies at the ready—the hidden, faith-filled wheat from the papistic chaff, so to speak."

New Fuel for Liturgy Wars

Francis himself used the word "irreversible" in August 2017 when he spoke on the most controversial of all the changes that Catholics experienced in the years following Vatican II: the dramatic alterations in the language and rubrics of the Mass. Speaking to a conference in

Italy, the pope stressed that the changes wrought by the council could not be undone.

The pope—who, unlike his predecessor Benedict XVI, had rarely spoken about liturgical matters—argued that the post-conciliar changes were not sudden. They were part of a long history of reform, he said, that dated back to the early years of the twentieth century. Those changes, he continued, responded "to real needs and to the concrete hopes of a renewal." Therefore, he concluded, "we can assert with certainty and magisterial authority that the liturgy reform is irreversible."

Francis has been reluctant to invoke his magisterial authority on doctrinal questions, but here he invoked it in connection with liturgical reform. Once again his words were profoundly confusing. The pope said in the same address that liturgical renewal is a continuing process. What does it mean to speak with "magisterial authority" about a *process*?

Virtually every Catholic, from the crustiest traditionalist to the most iconoclastic radical, would agree that *something* should be done to the liturgy. Hardly anyone is satisfied with the current state of liturgical affairs. The only questions are whether, how, and in which direction the process should continue.

Insofar as he was saying that the Church is committed to the process that began with Vatican II, Francis was only reinforcing what John Paul II and Benedict XVI had said. But many analysts who read the pope's speech—including, notably, those who applauded it most enthusiastically—interpreted his words as a distinct break from the statements of his immediate predecessors. Father Anthony Ruff, an influential American liturgist, remarked, "It is obvious just what, and who, is omitted." Ruff did not spell it out, but he clearly meant that Francis never mentioned his predecessor, Benedict XVI, who had written and spoken so frequently about the liturgy. The implication was that with this major address the current pope had thrust aside the ideas of the former pope, who had always emphasized the need for continuity in the Church's teaching and worship.

But if Pope Francis is free to discard the ideas of Pope Benedict, then a future pope should be free to discard the ideas of Pope Francis. And if Francis was indeed reversing the policies of his immediate predecessor, he was, in the process, undermining the supposed irreversibility of his own policies.

Three weeks later Francis took another bold step forward on the liturgical battlefield with a *motu proprio* giving national bishops' conferences the authority—previously reserved to the Holy See—to prepare and approve vernacular translations of liturgical texts. On paper, *Magnum Principium* involves only a minor shift in jurisdiction. But the pope's move is likely to have far-reaching effects in practice, possibly reigniting the battles over translations that were fought with particular vigor in the English-speaking world in the 1990s.

In 2001, the Congregation for Divine Worship and the Discipline of the Sacraments released the instruction *Liturgiam Authenticam* providing guidelines for liturgical translations. That instruction—which called upon translators to adhere as closely as possible to the language of original Latin texts—remains in effect. *Magnum Principium*, however, was hailed by critics of *Liturgiam Authenticam* as grounds for a reconsideration of the fundamental principles of translation and an effort to produce new English-language versions of the liturgy.

Actually, Francis does *not* suggest new approaches to translation. Quite on the contrary, in his *motu proprio* he states that the existing Vatican instructions "were and remain at the level of general guidelines and, as far as possible, must be followed by liturgical commissions.... " Still the overall effect of the new papal document was to reopen a painful debate within the Catholic community.

An Odd Affinity for Traditionalists?

Francis seems to be working directly against the goal of "irreversible change" with one important policy initiative: his drive to regularize the status of the Society of St. Pius X (SSPX), a traditionalist group that broke with Rome in 1988 when its founder, Archbishop Marcel Lefebvre, defied the Holy See in consecrating four bishops. All the bishops involved in that ceremony incurred the penalty of excommunication, and the SSPX priests they ordained were never accorded canonical status. Benedict XVI lifted the excommunications in 2009, but the status of SSPX clerics remained irregular; they did not have official permission to administer the Sacraments.

During most of Benedict's pontificate the Vatican engaged in negotiations with the SSPX, hoping to bring its followers back into the fold. The talks stalled, however, when the leaders of the group balked at acknowledging the validity of the teachings of Vatican II. Francis surprised many observers by continuing the talks, going even further to achieve a reconciliation. In 2015 he granted SSPX priests the authority to hear sacramental confessions, and in 2017 he announced that the Catholic Church would accept the validity of marriages at which an SSPX priest presided.

As I write, informed sources in Rome say that it is only a matter of time before the Vatican fully recognizes the SSPX, making it a personal prelature. The prelature would exercise authority over SSPX priests, ensuring that they were not subject to disciplinary control by diocesan bishops unsympathetic to the traditionalist movement. By all accounts, the Vatican has already offered the SSPX this status. The sticking point seems to be a requirement that the SSPX acknowledge the authority of Vatican II, but Francis has reportedly made concessions far beyond those offered by Benedict, including an acknowledgement that there can be legitimate differences of opinion as to the authority and the interpretation of the council documents.

Why would a pontiff bent on radical change within the Church make this extraordinary effort to reconcile with recalcitrant traditionalists? Suspicious members of the SSPX are asking exactly that question. Is the proposed reconciliation a tactic to bring the traditionalists to heel, to regain the disciplinary leverage that the Vatican lost when the SSPX leaders were excommunicated? Or is an SSPX prelature seen as a sort of ecclesiastical safety valve, a way for "rigid" Catholics to segregate themselves, leaving dioceses and parishes to the ministrations of the new liberal hegemony?

There is a simple explanation, really, which has three parts. First, Francis has always said that the Church should reach out to those on the "peripheries," and the SSPX is undeniably on the periphery of Catholicism today. Second, traditionalism has demonstrated an enduring appeal. Once thought to be the last gasp of a resistance that would die out as its members aged, the movement has attracted thousands of young Catholics. In France today, traditionalist chapels draw more worshippers than ordinary parishes. Third, and most important, the sticking point in negotiations with the SSPX has always been the group's hesitance about Vatican II, and Francis has never been overly worried about the details of doctrine, discipline, and "the law."

The Lessons of China and Venezuela

The willingness to overlook difficulties in doctrine has also been an important factor in negotiations between the Vatican and the People's Republic of China. On that front too, rumors suggest that an imminent accord will end a longstanding impasse over the appointment of new Catholic bishops in China. But if the rumors are true, the price of that agreement could be a crucial concession to Beijing, a concession that Benedict XVI had firmly ruled out.

For decades, the Holy See has wrangled with the communist regime over control of the Church in China. The government insists that the Church must be under the guidance of the Communist Party through the government-controlled Catholic Patriotic Association. Benedict maintained that a role for the Patriotic Association cannot be reconciled with the freedom of the Church. There matters stood, apparently at a stalemate, during Benedict's reign. The Patriotic Association appointed several bishops, whose consecrations the Holy See regarded as illicit. The Chinese government, for its part, refused to recognize the "underground" Catholic bishops, whose appointments had not been authorized by the regime. Many if not most Chinese bishops have managed to win approval from both the government and the Holy See, but the process for doing so is murky, the situation unstable. "Underground" Catholics are subject to police harassment, and bishops are under heavy pressure to bow to the Patriotic Association.

Under Francis, there have been signs that the stalemate could be broken, and the Vatican is reportedly ready to offer a new compromise: the Holy See would appoint new bishops, but it would select them from a list of candidates prepared by Chinese authorities. Thus the Holy See would protect its claim to ultimate authority over appointments, while Beijing could exclude clerics who were deemed unfriendly to the government.

Cardinal Joseph Zen, the retired bishop of Hong Kong, who for years has been the leading Catholic critic of the mainland government, fears the Vatican is "going to make a very bad agreement with China." The rumored agreement, he says, would "give too much decision-making power to the government." Loyal Catholics could easily be excluded from consideration for appointment as bishops, and it is "really naïve," he warns, to think that the Communist Party would hesitate to use that leverage.

Cardinal Zen has disclosed that he has frequently written to the pontiff expressing his concerns, but "he doesn't answer my letters." To compound the problem, "the people around him are not good at all."

Shortly after the Chinese cardinal's lament, the head of the Catholic Patriotic Association, Liu Bainian, essentially confirmed Zen's fears that the accord would "sell out the underground Church," telling the *South China Morning Post* that the government would not recognize the "underground" bishops. He was responding to reports that after a deal was struck, the Holy See would recognize the bishops who had been selected by the Patriotic Association and consecrated illicitly, while the regime would recognize the "underground" bishops. Scoffing at that notion, Liu said, "There's no such proposal being heard on the mainland yet." The Vatican must recognize the regime's bishops, he said, but those prelates who had not sought the approval of the government are "unfit for the people to work with."

A prudent negotiator knows when to make a dramatic offer and when to take a stand on principle. Francis, however, typically betrays his anxiety to reach an agreement regardless of the cost, a weakness that undermined an effort in 2016 to mediate an escalating dispute between the Venezuelan government and opposition leaders.

The socialist regime of Nicolás Maduro was responsible for a crushing economic crisis in Venezuela, and unrest was building. Cardinal Pietro Parolin, the Vatican Secretary of State, said that the Holy See would mediate talks between the government and opposition if certain conditions were met: the government must free political prisoners, allow humanitarian agencies to deliver food and medicine to those in need, and schedule new elections. The government did not fulfill any of those conditions, the opposition withdrew from talks, and the negotiations soon collapsed.

The Venezuelan bishops had sparred for years with Maduro and his predecessor, Hugo Chávez, criticizing both rulers for their strong-arm tactics. In reply both Chávez and Maduro had charged that the bishops were in league with the opposition and accused the hierarchy of sedition. Now Maduro stepped up his anticlerical rhetoric, and bands of the president's supporters threatened bishops and vandalized cathedrals. In the summer of 2017 the Venezuelan bishops warned that their country was becoming a "totalitarian, militarist, violent, oppressive police-state system." They released a prayer to the Virgin Mary to "free our country from the clutches of communism and socialism."

And how did the pope respond to this assault on democracy and intimidation of Catholic prelates? In April 2017, Francis told reporters that he was hoping dialogue would resolve the problems in Venezuela, but "part of the opposition does not want this." He did not mention the government's responsibility for the breakdown in talks. In a letter to the Venezuelan bishops the pope sounded the same forlorn hope: "I am convinced that the serious problems of Venezuela can be solved if there is the will to build bridges, if you want to talk seriously and adhere to agreements reached." Perversely, Maduro used the pope's public statements against the bishops, charging that the prelates were out of touch with Rome.

Despite his frequent calls for decentralizing Church leadership, in both China and Venezuela Francis has distanced himself from the public stands of local prelates. In the case of Venezuela, the pontiff's own political preferences might explain his failure to support the bishops. Chávez and Maduro styled themselves as leaders of a "popular movement," insisting that they were fighting for the people against powerful elites—a posture that appeals to Francis. As the crisis came to a head in May 2017, an Italian political scientist, Loris Zanatta, suggested that the pope is dangerously subject to the lure of ideology:

> Reality, Bergoglio repeats, is greater than ideas. And yet, seeing his silence on the social drama in Venezuela, or in the country that with Chávez had set itself up as a model of anti-liberalism by invoking the stereotypes dear to the Pope, the thought arises that he too, like many, prefers his ideas to reality.

The Challenge of Islamic Extremism

Something similar could be said about the pope's refusal to acknowledge the unique threat of Islamic terrorism. Francis speaks out frequently on behalf of persecuted Christians, especially in the Middle East, but he seems to ignore the obvious connection between Islamic regimes and religious oppression. On the contrary, at every available opportunity he insists that Islam, like every other religion, opposes violence. On several occasions he has argued that terrorism is the product of a global economic system based on profit rather than a religious doctrine based on conquest.

In an interview with the French newspaper *La Croix* in May 2016, Francis went further, denying that the people of Europe are worried about Islamic terrorism. "I do not think there is now a fear of Islam, as such, but of *Daesh* [the Islamic State] and its war of conquest," he said. He did admit that the Islamic State is "driven in part by Islam," but then he hastened to make the case that the exploitation of religion for the purpose of violence is not peculiar to Islam: "The idea of conquest is inherent in the soul of Islam, it is true. But it could be interpreted with the same idea of conquest [found at] the end of the Gospel of Matthew, where Jesus sends his disciples in all nations."

Was the bishop of Rome actually saying that Christ's Great Commission is comparable to the ideology of jihad? Incredible as it seems, that interpretation would be consistent with other statements he has made. While some Islamic fundamentalists are a threat to society, he has allowed, Christianity has its fundamentalists as well. Is he suggesting that the "rigid" Catholics whose views he so often denounces, the "fundamentalists," are potentially as dangerous as jihadist warriors? It seems preposterous that a Roman pontiff would make such an argument, yet his words speak for themselves.

In his famous Regensburg address in September 2006, Benedict XVI provided a framework for the critical evaluation of Islam, insisting that Muslim leaders must address the tendency to resolve disputes by force rather than reason. At the time, Cardinal Bergoglio explicitly distanced himself from the pope's line of reasoning, denying that Benedict spoke for him. The Regensburg address, of course, provoked an angry reaction from the Muslim world, while Bergoglio's determination not to give offense won him friends there. But a decade later, the logic of the Regensburg address remains persuasive.

Benedict insisted on upholding both the law of reason and the reason behind the law. In contrast, Francis expresses contempt for the "doctors of the law." This is not merely a difference of style.

Reverence for the Law

In his written statements and public appearances, Francis has often spoken with warmth and obvious love about the beauties of the Catholic Faith. But he has rarely, if ever, spoken about the love for God's Law that rings throughout the Old Testament. Psalm 119 offers only one of many examples:

> Oh, how I love thy law!
> Thy commandment makes me wiser than my enemies,
> for it is ever with me.
> I have more understanding than all my teachers,
> for thy testimonies are my meditation (Ps. 119:97–99).

To meditate on the Law, probing deeply into its wisdom, was seen by the Psalmist as a great blessing. The revelation of the Law unlocked the secrets of the universe. The more one understood the Law, the more one could live in harmony with creation. In the modern era we rejoice when scientific research deepens our comprehension of nature's laws. So it is with *the* Law, God's Law, which includes but is not limited to the law of nature. And so it was that the people of Israel, of whom Christians are spiritual heirs, boasted that when God revealed his Law to them, he showed them special favor. "He has not dealt thus with any other nation; they do not know his ordinances. Praise the Lord!" (Ps. 147:20)

Needless to say, the laws of the Church—canon law—do not occupy the same exalted position as the immutable Law of God. They are an attempt by fallen human beings to codify the practical applications of *the* Law to ordinary life. They can change, whereas *the* Law cannot— just as speed limits and tax rates can change, but the law of gravity or the principle of non-contradiction cannot. But even these man-made laws deserve respect, as they represent the accumulated wisdom of the universal Church, put to the service of God's work on Earth.

Much of the Code of Canon Law reflects the fruit of painful experience. That is how laws commonly come into being, actually, both in the Church and in the secular world. Legislators identify a problem or an abuse, propose a solution, and write it into law. If the solution is effective the problem is eased. If not, future legislators will probably take another stab at it. Thus law can be the codification of common sense: practical problems are recognized and remedies applied—often after a painful process of trial and error.

Quite a bit of the Church's pastoral wisdom falls into this category: not necessarily lofty theology, but the fruit of experience. Wise pastors find a good way to address a knotty problem, suggest the same solution to others, and eventually the Church in her wisdom declares that everyone should follow that same path.

Activists are impatient with rules. They have plans and they want results—now! If their plan of action is stymied by existing law, their first instinct is to cast the law aside, especially if they cannot see why the law is necessary. But *their* failure to understand the purpose of the law does not mean that the law *has* no purpose. Quite possibly the legislator understood something that the activist has not yet grasped. It's even possible that the law was written after the failure of a plan like the one the activist now has in mind.

Obviously there are times when a law should be amended, abolished, or even defied. But before setting the law aside, one should understand why it was written and the likely consequences of discarding it. Church law, developed and refined over the centuries, represents a storehouse of wisdom about human nature and human frailty. The canons are there for a reason. Should some canons be changed? No doubt. But they should not be ignored.

With his repeated criticisms of "the doctors of the law," Francis suggests an opposition between those who enforce the law and those who dispense mercy, between canon law and pastoral practice. Not so. It is a fundamental principle of Church law that the welfare of souls is the supreme law. Every canon, therefore, should be interpreted from the perspective of a conscientious pastor. The code is designed to help pastors: to guide them, not to limit them.

The "Democracy of the Dead"

With his willingness to set aside the constraints of the law in favor of a spontaneous new approach, Francis has undoubtedly gained favor with the secular world. Four years into his pontificate he continues to enjoy wide popularity in spite of the controversies that he has provoked. But has the "Francis effect" brought any lasting benefits to the Catholic Church? The available statistics suggest otherwise.

After years of decline, the number of Catholic priests in the world began to increase in 2000, rising slightly each year until 2015, when it declined. The number of young priests is a lagging indicator of sorts, since the young men who are ordained this year were attracted to the priestly ministry several years ago. So it is even more revealing to see the statistics on seminary enrollment. There the number rose after 2000, peaked in 2011 and 2012, and then began to decline. It would be simplistic to blame the drop on Francis. But the figures contradict the myth that the "Francis effect" has sparked a revival.

Would it be surprising if, after an initial burst of enthusiasm, young Catholics did not respond to the appeal of a pontiff who broke with the time-honored teachings of the Church? The Catholic Faith is not merely a collection of propositions for belief; it is also a set of traditions built up over the generations, a heritage that the faithful come to cherish.

By scorning traditions and scoffing at canon law, Francis is not only provoking divisions within the Catholic Church of the early twenty-first century but also breaking the continuity between today's Catholics and their forefathers in the Faith. G. K. Chesterton wrote about the "democracy of the dead," arguing that our ancestors should have their say in contemporary affairs, that we should respect the wisdom and the wishes of those who prepared the way for us with their sacrifices and their prayers. If the Catholic Faith today is not the Faith of our great-great-grandparents—if it is not the Faith of the apostles and martyrs—what is it?

With his words and actions, Francis has devalued the work of his predecessors and thus diminished the teaching office of the papacy. If a Catholic today is free to ignore the teachings of John Paul II, as Francis implies, then a Catholic tomorrow will be free to ignore the teachings of Francis. The only escape from this dilemma is the one suggested by Benedict XVI: the hermeneutic of continuity. Papal teachings must be interpreted, and a pope's pastoral initiatives should be judged, in continuity with two thousand years of Catholic tradition. By that standard, the papacy of Francis has been a disaster for the Church.

"We have no means of knowing how far a small mistake in the faith may carry us astray," wrote John Henry Newman. The great nineteenth-century English theologian, beatified by Benedict XVI in 2010, argued forcefully against a way of thinking that is familiar to anyone who has heard Francis ridicule the "doctors of the law":

> It is a fashion of the day, then, to suppose that all insisting upon precise Articles of Faith is injurious to the cause of spiritual religion, and inconsistent with an enlightened view of it; that it is all one to maintain, that the Gospel requires the reception of definite and positive Articles, and to acknowledge it to be technical and formal; that such a notion is superstitious, and interferes with the "liberty wherewith Christ has made us free;" that it argues a deficient insight into the principles and ends, a narrow comprehension of the spirit of His Revelation.

Newman contrasts that fashionable view with St. Paul's exhortation to the Christians at Ephesus to hold fast to the Deposit of Faith. The responsibility of proclaiming God's Word fully and accurately weighed heavily on the apostle, who knew its saving power and the deadly danger of turning from the truth. "And so I solemnly declare to you this day," he told the Ephesians, "that I am innocent of the blood of all of you, for I did not shrink from declaring to you the whole counsel of God" (Acts 20:26–27).

Can the Pope Be Wrong?

Pious Catholics rarely criticize the man they recognize as the Vicar of Christ. In the fourteenth century, St. Catherine of Siena referred to the bishop of Rome as the "sweet Christ on Earth." Yet this feisty doctor of the Church did not shrink from reproving Pope Gregory XI to his face for continuing the exile of the papal court in Avignon.

But *can* the pope be wrong? Or more importantly, can the wrong man occupy the chair of Peter? Again, some pious Catholics assume that with the Holy Spirit guiding the Church, it is impossible for a conclave to choose the wrong man. If only that were the case! When Cardinal Joseph Ratzinger was asked in 1990 if the Holy Spirit chooses the Roman pontiff, the future pope responded,

> I would not say so, in the sense that the Holy Spirit picks out the Pope. ... I would say that the Spirit does not exactly take control of the affair, but rather like a good educator, as it were, leaves us much space, much freedom, without entirely abandoning us. Thus the Spirit's role should be understood in a much more elastic sense, not that he dictates the candidate for whom one must vote. Probably the only assurance he offers is that the thing cannot be totally ruined. There are too many contrary instances of popes the Holy Spirit obviously would not have picked!

The Catholic Church teaches that the occupant of Peter's throne has the authority to pronounce infallible teachings. But that power can be invoked only under certain circumstances. The First Vatican Council, which in 1870 defined the doctrine of papal infallibility in the dogmatic constitution *Pastor Aeternus*, made it clear that this extraordinary papal power is not a special license to amend Catholic teaching: "For the Holy Spirit was promised to the successors of Peter not so that they might, by his revelation, make known some new doctrine, but that, by his assistances, they might religiously guard and faithfully expound the revelation or deposit of faith transmitted by the apostles" (4:4.6).

The Dominican theologian Aidan Nichols warns that the implication in *Amoris Laetitia* that "actions condemned by the law of Christ can sometimes be morally right or even, indeed, requested by God" has caused "extremely grave" confusion and could lead to the unprecedented situation in which the Church "tolerated concubinage." His concern is so deep that he has proposed adding to the Code of Canon Law "a procedure for calling to order a Pope who teaches error."

There is no provision in the current Code of Canon Law for correcting papal error, but the First Vatican Council, Father Nichols observes, did not take the position "that a Pope is incapable of leading people astray." A canonical procedure for the correction of a pope might deter novelties in papal teaching and reassure non-Catholic Christians who are suspicious of sweeping papal authority. "Indeed," he says, "it may be that the present crisis of the Roman magisterium is providentially intended to call attention to the limits of primacy in this regard."

In his homily at the Mass inaugurating his papacy in May 2005, Benedict XVI reflected on the limits of papal authority:

> The Pope is not an absolute monarch whose thoughts and desires are law. On the contrary: the Pope's ministry is a guarantee of obedience to Christ and to his Word. He must not proclaim his own ideas, but rather constantly bind himself and the Church to obedience to God's Word, in the face of every attempt to adapt it or water it down, and every form of opportunism.

The Moral Duty of Bishops

All Christians—not just the pope—have the duty to cling to the Word of God, preserving the integrity of the Faith, but bishops, the primary teachers of the Faith, have a special obligation. If the pope is spreading unrest and confusion, local bishops must allay the fears of the faithful and restore clarity.

Even if Pope Francis is not personally responsible for the confusion that now prevails—even if his teaching is perfectly sound, but some people have misinterpreted it—other bishops are morally obliged to step in. The undeniable differences within the college of bishops must be resolved for the sake of the integrity of the Faith.

Unfortunately, few bishops have acknowledged the divisions opened up by this pontificate. Although scores of them, recognizing the confusion caused by conflicting interpretations, have quietly expressed misgivings about *Amoris Laetitia*, only four cardinals were willing to sign a public call for clarification. Cardinal Kevin Farrell, the prefect of the Vatican's new Dicastery for Laity, Family, and Life, told a reporter in 2017 that of all the bishops who have met with him during their visits to Rome, "no one had anything negative" to say about the papal document.

Perhaps these bishops fear that the pope will retaliate against anyone who challenges him, or that public opposition will weaken the prestige of the papacy. But the papacy is weakened when one pontiff contradicts another. The damage done by Francis cannot be repaired unless it is recognized. Denying problems and papering over the differences only amplifies the confusion.

It is not enough to say that *Amoris Laetitia* should be read in the context of constant Church teaching if the intention behind the document is to change Church teaching. Several American bishops have gone out of their way to praise the solid portions of *Amoris Laetitia* while skipping lightly past the problems of the notorious eighth chapter. That diplomatic approach, too, is confusing, because the document has been so widely interpreted as a break from the magisterial tradition.

Yes, there are some fine passages in *Amoris Laetitia*. But on the whole it fails as a teaching document because, as the saying goes, what is good is not new, and what is new is not good. St. John Paul II enriched the Magisterium on marriage and family life incalculably with a body of teaching innovative in its approach yet fully in accord with the constant traditions of the Church. Francis's apostolic exhortation has undermined that teaching so seriously that now, only a dozen years after John Paul's death, we face the task of rebuilding it from the ground up—a vexing waste of effort at a time when this teaching is so desperately needed.

The Role of the Laity

How can loyal Catholics help to restore Catholic unity while we wait for stronger leadership by our bishops?

First, foremost, and always, by prayer. The pope needs the whole-hearted support of the faithful when he promotes the constant teaching of the Church. When he does not, the faithful should pray that he will change his approach. Pray that the pope will lead the Church toward greater unity. If he must change his approach in order to do that, so be it. Stranger things have happened.

Pray, too, for the next pope. Whoever he is and whenever he will ascend Peter's throne, he will face a prodigious task of restoring unity of faith and clarity of teaching while pursuing the necessary but unfinished work of Vatican reform. If he approaches that task boldly, he will encounter opposition, disobedience, and the threat of schism. Unlike Francis, he will not enjoy the sympathy of the non-Catholic world and the secular media. A good pontiff, striving to clear up the muddle that Francis is likely to leave behind, will have to rely solely on the help of the faithful.

For now, calls for the pope's resignation are futile. He is not likely to step down. Even if he did, the presence of *two* former pontiffs—one with a record of imprudent public remarks—would guarantee further confusion. The challenge is to preserve the teaching authority of the papacy, not to dilute it.

Nor is it useful to look to Benedict XVI to allay the reigning confusion. The retired pontiff, determined to live out his remaining years in silence, has taken a vow of fidelity to his successor; he will not and should not violate that vow. He knows that any comment he makes about Vatican affairs, no matter how innocuous, will be scrutinized for the subtlest disagreement with the current pope. The counsel of the greatest living Catholic theologian would surely be invaluable, yet Benedict is the very last Catholic who can offer his opinions today.

The Catholic Church holds that a Roman pontiff is infallible when, in union with the world's bishops, he solemnly defines Catholic teaching on faith and morals. Francis has eschewed formal definitions, preferring impromptu comments. His most enthusiastic supporters, who in the past have been notably skeptical about papal authority, now demand that the faithful ascribe magisterial weight even to the pope's offhand comments. But if an offhand comment appears to contradict the formal teaching of a previous pontiff, they cannot *both* be right. So the confusion grows. The magisterial confusion of this papacy has, strangely enough, expanded the claims of papal infallibility—often invoked where it does not apply—while weakening its foundations.

No precept of the Faith compels Catholics to believe that the Roman pontiff is always wise in his judgments, prudent in his statements, and clear in his thinking. Nor, of course, do questionable statements by one pope call into question the whole history of Catholic teaching. The Church has survived uncertain leadership in the past and, with the certain promise of God's grace, can weather the latest storm.

A proper understanding of the limits of papal authority would help to resolve the current crisis. The bishop of Rome is not a solitary potentate but the leader of the College of Bishops. The Second Vatican Council's dogmatic constitution on the Church, *Lumen Gentium*, explains,

"Just as the office which the Lord confided to Peter alone, as first of the apostles, destined to be transmitted to his successors, is a permanent one, so also endures the office, which the apostles received, of shepherding the Church, a charge destined to be exercised without interruption by the sacred order of bishops." If the pope himself has gone astray, the duty falls upon the other shepherds to bring the Church back to safe pastures.

Pope Francis has not taught heresy, but the confusion he has stirred up has destabilized the universal Church. The faithful have been led to question themselves, their beliefs, their Faith. They look to Rome for guidance and instead find more questions, more confusion.

For thirty-five years, loyal Catholics were accustomed to looking to Rome for guidance, to ease the confusion that arose from uncertain leadership at the local level. Now the situation has been reversed, particularly in the United States. Some American bishops have become bolder in their defenses of orthodoxy, more willing to risk the disapproval of the secular world. Today they need the encouragement of faithful Catholics, as their duty requires them to risk disapproval from Rome.

Index

A

abortion, 15–16, 26, 30, 34, 74, 118, 163–64, 166–68

Administration of the Patrimony of the Apostolic See (APSA), 49, 55–56, 59–60

Africa, Africans, 4, 90–93, 124, 158, 170

Allen, John, 40, 43, 85, 101, 131, 151

Amoris Laetitia, xi, 113–20, 124–26, 128–46, 158–59, 161, 192–94

annulment, 76, 96, 100–2, 119

Apostolic Signatura, 77, 82, 144, 151

Apuron, Anthony, 63

Aquinas, Thomas, 24, 139

B

Bagnasco, Angelo, 89

Baldisseri, Lorenzo, 81, 84, 87

Bambino Gesù Hospital, 69–70

Bandera, Gianantonio, 70

Barros, Juan, 63

Beijing, 146, 182–83

Benedict XVI, xii, 1–2, 4, 8, 11, 15, 20, 22, 24, 39–40, 42, 48, 52, 62, 75, 89, 102, 111, 134, 144, 146, 148, 161, 165, 169, 171–72, 176, 179, 181–82, 186, 190, 192, 195

Bergoglio, Jorge, 6–8, 14–15, 18, 148–52, 156–57, 165, 169, 185–86

Bertone, Tarcisio, 69–70

Brandmüller, Walter, 126, 128, 144

Buenos Aires, 7, 14, 16, 18, 124, 151, 165

Burke, Raymond, 77, 82–83, 85, 95, 126, 128, 144, 151, 159

Buttiglione, Rocco, 121–23

C

Caffarra, Carlo, 107, 126, 128–29, 144

Capozzi, Luigi, 70–71

Castel Gandolfo, 4, 8

Catechism of the Catholic Church, xiv, 29, 80, 122

Catholic Herald, 65

Catholic World Report, 95

Celestine V, 2

Cervellera, Bernardo, 147

Chaouqui, Francesca, 49–51

climate change, 24–26, 28, 165–66

Coccopalmerio, Francesco, 70, 138

Code of Canon Law, 65, 100, 126, 167–68, 188, 192

Coleridge, Mark, 129–31

College of Cardinals, 5, 39, 53, 56, 74–75, 128, 150, 169–71

Collins, Charles, 47

Collins, Marie, 66–69

Collins, Thomas, 107

Congregation for Divine Worship and the Discipline of the Sacraments, 180

Congregation for the Doctrine of the Faith, 40, 44, 64, 66, 82, 128, 138–39, 155, 161, 164

Conley, James, 24

contraception, contraceptives, 16, 32–34, 74, 80, 118, 163, 166, 177–78

Crux, 47, 85, 131, 139, 151

Cupich, Blase, 132, 170

D

Danneels, Godfried, 64, 148–50

Degollado, Marcial Maciel, 40

Deposit of Faith, xi–xiv, 95, 140, 143, 190, 192

Dicastery for Laity, Family, and Life, 44, 193

Dicastery for Promoting Integral Human Development, 44

Dolan, Timothy, 80, 107

dubia, 126, 128–36, 138, 141, 151, 158

E

Eighth Chapter of the Post-Synodal Apostolic Exhortation Amoris Laetitia, The, 138

Eijk, Willem, 107
environmentalism, 16, 28
Erdő, Péter, 86, 88, 93, 104, 107
Eucharist, the, xii, 74, 87, 98, 102,
    121, 123–26, 129, 138, 154
Evangelii Gaudium, 21–24
extraordinary synod, 77

F

Familiaris Consortio, 87, 99, 119,
    125
Fernández, Victor Manuel, 139,
    177
Fessio, Joseph, 26, 83, 166
Fiat Lux, 28
Figueroa, Marcelo, 165
Finland, 178
First Vatican Council, 191–92
Fisichella, Rino, 20, 28, 167
Fittipaldi, Emiliano, 48–50
"Francis effect," the, ix, 15–16, 37,
    177, 189

G

Gabriele, Paolo, 3
Gadecki, Stanislaw, 86
Gagliarducci, Andrea, 52–53
Galantino, Nunzio, 164–65
Galeazzi, Giacomo, 145–46

gender ideology, 34–35, 79, 105
Gómez, José, 170
Guénois, Jean-Marie, 37, 43, 139

H

hermeneutic of continuity, 176,
    178, 190
Holy Communion, x, 82, 87,
    89–91, 94, 98–101, 107, 110,
    113, 115, 118–19, 121–27, 129,
    134, 138, 141–42, 164
homosexuality, 17, 91–93, 118
Honduras, 158
Humanae Vitae, 79–80, 177–78

I

Ignatius Press, 77, 83, 166
Institute for Religious Works, 2, 40
Islam, 91, 134, 185–86
Ivereigh, Austen, 137, 143, 149

J

Jesuits, 15, 151–52, 157, 175, 178
John XXIII, 9, 26, 171
John Paul II, xii, 2, 4, 23, 40, 52,
    56, 86–87, 89, 99, 111, 116, 119,
    121, 125, 127, 133, 144, 148,
    162–63, 165, 169, 171–72, 175–
    77, 179, 190, 194
Jubilee Year of Mercy, 168

K

Kasper, Walter, 74–77, 82–83, 87, 90–92, 98–100, 102–3, 110–11, 114–15, 118, 123–24, 137, 140, 148, 161, 163–64, 169

"Kasper proposal," the, 74, 76–77, 83, 87, 90–91, 99–100, 102–3, 110–11, 114–15, 118, 123–24, 137, 140, 161, 163–64

Knights of Malta, x, 151

Krakow, 56, 175

L

La Civiltà Cattolica, 105, 120–21, 134, 165

La Repubblica, 18–19

La Stampa, 88, 125, 145

Laudato Si', 24–28, 108, 139

L'Espresso, 16, 106

Lauri, Omero, 169

"law of gradualness," 75, 99

Lefebvre, Marcel, 181

Le Figaro, 37, 43, 139

Lehmann, Karl, 148

LifeSite News, 26, 163, 166

Liturgiam Authenticam, 180

Lombardi, Federico, 5, 19, 47, 75, 84, 92, 155

L'Osservatore Romano, 46, 121

Lumen Fidei, 20–21, 24

Lumen Gentium, 195

M

Maduro, Nicolás, 184–85

Magister, Sandro, 16–17, 32, 34, 106–9

Magisterium, the, 20, 26, 73, 94, 97, 113, 120, 131–33, 139, 141, 166, 194

Magnum Principium, 180

Maio, Nicola, 49–50

Maradiaga, Rodríguez, 158–59, 165

marriage, xii, 16, 34, 74–80, 86–90, 94–102, 106, 114–19, 122, 124–26, 129, 135, 138, 141, 144, 154, 162, 165, 177, 181, 194

Martin, James, 105

Martini, Carlo, 148

Marx, Reinhard, 76, 90, 133, 159, 169

McCarrick, Theodore, 149–50, 169

McShea, Bronwen Catherine, 178

Meisner, Joachim, 126, 128, 144

Mettepenningen, Jürgen, 148

Milone, Libero, 59–61

motu proprio, 59, 65, 180

Müller, Gerhard, 66–68, 82–83, 88, 107–8, 126, 128–29, 138, 144, 161–62, 165

Murphy-O'Connor, Cormac, 148–50

N

Napier, Wilfrid, 85–86, 107, 124

National Catholic Register, 57, 60, 110, 132–33, 139

National Catholic Reporter, 171

new evangelization, the, 4, 6, 20, 22, 89

Newman, John Henry, 190

Nichols, Aidan, 192

Nuzzi, Gianluigi, 48–50

O

O'Malley, Sean, 64–65, 67–68

P

Paglia, Vincenzo, 162–63

Pakaluk, Michael, 139–40

Papale, Claudio, 67

Parolin, Pietro, 48, 184

Pastor Aeternus, 192

Patriotic Association, 182–83

Paul VI, 9, 33, 73, 79, 177

Pell, George, 50–54, 56–57, 59–61, 84–85, 88, 94, 107, 109–10, 128, 130

Pentin, Edward, 60, 84, 91–92, 132, 139

People's Republic of China, 182

Piacenza, Mauro, 107, 150–51

Pinto, Pio Vito, 128

Pontifical Academy for Life, 162–64, 178

Pontifical Academy of Sciences, 26

Pontifical Council for Christian Unity, 74

Pontifical Council for Social Communications, 46

Pontifical John Paul II Institute for Studies on Marriage and the Family, 144, 177

PricewaterhouseCoopers, 57–59

Profiti, Giuseppe, 69

R

Ratzinger, Joseph, 4, 7, 15, 40, 100, 148, 191. *See also Benedict XVI*

Reese, Thomas, 106, 171–72

Regensburg address, 134, 186

relation, 85–89, 93–95

Remaining in the Truth of Christ, 83–84

Ricca, Battista, 16–17

Rigging of a Vatican Synod, The, 84

Roman Curia, 6, 39–45, 48, 51, 53–54, 57–58, 61, 66–68, 107, 150, 155, 171

Roman Rota, 79, 128

Rosica, Thomas, 105

Royal, Robert, 82, 93, 119

S

Sacrament of Penance, the, 87, 127, 142, 168

same-sex unions, 74, 78, 88, 95

Sarah, Robert, 88, 93, 105, 107

Saunders, Peter, 66

Savino, Jorge Urosa, 107

Scalfari, Eugenio, 18–19

Scarano, Nunzio, 55–56

Schelkens, Karim, 148,

Schmitz, Matthew, 156

Schönborn, Christoph, 115, 125, 131, 141–44

Scola, Angelo, 4, 107

Second Vatican Council, 32, 73, 87, 106, 146, 173, 195

Secretariat for the Economy, 41, 50–53, 57–61, 65

Secretariat of State, 44, 47–48, 57–58, 105, 121

sede vacante period, 5

sex-abuse scandal, 2, 6, 58, 61, 68

Silvestrini, Achille, 148

Society of St. Pius X (SSPX), 181

Sorondo, Marcelo Sánchez, 26, 166

Spadaro, Antonio, 93, 105, 120–21, 131, 134–35, 140–41, 152, 165

Spina, Massimo, 69

St. Augustine, 24, 122

St. Gallen mafia, 147–50

St. Martha's residence, 10, 14

St. Peter, xi, xiii-xiv, 10, 31, 37, 143, 154–55

St. Peter's Basilica, 1, 10–11, 28

Synod of Bishops, 22, 64, 73, 78, 80, 90, 97, 101, 110, 128, 132, 140–41

T

theology of the body, 86

Tobin, Joseph, 133, 170

Tornielli, Andrea, 51, 76, 125, 145–46

Trower, Philip, 174–75

Turmoil and Truth, 174

Twitter, 105, 131, 134

V

Vallejo Balda, Ángel, 49–51

Vatican Insider, 145–48

Vatican Radio, xii, 8, 14, 46–47, 67, 76, 86, 116

Vatileaks, 3, 6, 39, 48, 52

Vatileaks II, 48, 50–52, 56

Venezuela, 182, 184–85

Veritatis Splendor, 116, 127, 132, 140

Vigano, Dario, 46, 48

Vingt-Trois, André, 107

W

Weigel, George, 169

Wesolowski, Jósef, 62–63

Wuerl, Donald, 106

Z

Zanatta, Loris, 185

Zen, Joseph, 183